MAKE YOUR OWN
WORKBENCH

A Woodworker's Guide to Building the Right Bench for the Shop

From the Editors of

CEDAR LANE PRESS

CONTENTS

1. WORKBENCHES

2. ACCESSORIES

CONTRIBUTORS

TOOLS, SUPPLIES & RESOURCES

INDEX

1

WORKBENCHES

A bevy of benches to choose from. After familiarizing yourself with the basics (p. 6), take a look through the plans in this section to identify what style of bench will suit you best. There are classic designs, such as the Roubo and Scandinavian benches, as well as more modern choices meant for power tool work. Whether you seek a sturdy-but-frugal solution, a quick build, a knockdown option, a full-size heavy-duty bench, or maybe even something to pique your resident junior woodworker's interest, you'll find what you're looking for.

Holes for dogs to pinch work with end vise

End vise

Face of bench

Face vise

Holes for holdfasts to support long work

RULES FOR WORKBENCHES

These guidelines will help you make the most of your bench.

BY CHRISTOPHER SCHWARZ

When it comes to building or buying a bench, most woodworkers get wrapped up in what form it should take. Should it be a Continental bench popularized by Frank Klausz? A Shaker bench like the one at the Hancock community? How about a British version like Ian Kirby's?

Copying a well-known form is a natural tack to take. After all, when woodworkers buy or build their first workbench, they are in the early stages of learning the craft. They don't know what sort of bench or vises they need, or why one bench looks different than another. So they pick a form that looks good to them—occasionally mixing and matching bits and pieces from different forms—and get busy.

That, I believe, is the seed of the problem with workbenches today. Many commercial workbenches are missing key functions that make work-holding easier. And many classic bench forms get built with modifications that make them frustrating in use.

What's worse, the user might not even know that he or she is struggling. Woodworking is a solitary pursuit, and it's rare to use someone else's bench.

I've built a number of classic bench forms, and I've worked on craftsman-made and commercial benches of different stripes. I've been stunned by how awful some workbenches can be at some tasks, and I've also seen brilliantly realized designs.

And now, after all this work, I've concluded that it doesn't matter what sort of bench you have as long as it performs a set of core functions with ease.

DO YOU EVEN NEED A BENCH?

Before we get to the rules, it's fair to say that a lot of the best commercial woodworking today is done on benches that disregard many of these rules. In production shops, it's rare to find a traditional bench used in a traditional manner. More often, a commercial woodworker will have something akin to a clamping table, or even a door on sawhorses. And they can turn out high-quality work that will blow you away.

I once taught a class at a school where Thomas Stangeland, a maestro of Greene & Greene–inspired work, was also teaching a class. Though we both strive for the same result in craftsmanship, the processes we use

Big rig. This rig serves as the assembly bench in the *Popular Woodworking* shop, but if you put a vise on it somewhere, it probably could serve as a workbench in a production shop. It is simple and allows great flexibility for clamping. But some basic operations with this setup would be tricky.

couldn't be more different. He builds furniture for a living, and he enjoys it. I build furniture because I enjoy it, and I sell an occasional piece.

One evening we each gave a presentation to the students about our work and I showed an image of the enormous French workbench I'd built the year before and discussed its unusual history.

Thomas then got up and said he wished he had a picture of his workbench: a door on a couple horses. He said that a commercial shop had no time to waste on building a traditional bench. And with his power-tool approach, all he needs is a flat surface.

It's hard to argue with the end result. His furniture is beautiful.

But what's important here is that while you can build with the door-off-the-floor approach, there are many commercial woodworkers who still see the utility of a traditional workbench. Chairmaker and furniture maker Brian Boggs uses more

Too delicate. Spindly workbenches are nothing new. This anemic example from the early 20th century is too small and lacks mass. Sadly, there are modern ones that are even worse.

newfangled routers and shop-made devices with aluminum extrusions than I have ever seen. And he still has two enormous traditional workbenches that see constant use. Before Kelly Mehler opened a woodworking school, I visited his commercial shop and got a chance to inspect his vintage bench, which saw daily use.

The point is that a good bench won't make you a better woodworker, and a not-quite-a-bench won't doom you to failure. But a good bench will make many operations easier. It's simply a tool: the biggest clamp in the shop.

THE RULES

I've boiled down the core workbench functions into 10 rules for building (or buying) a workbench. As long as your bench obeys these rules (or most of them), you will be able to hold almost any workpiece for any task with a minimum of fuss. This will add speed and enjoyment to your time in the shop and reduce the amount of time you fuss with setups

Rule No. 1: Always Add Mass

Always overbuild your workbench by adding mass. There is a saying in boatbuilding: If it looks fair, it is fair. For workbenches, here's a maxim: If it looks stout, then make it doubly so. Everything about a workbench takes punishment that is akin to a kitchen chair in a house full of 8-year-old boys.

Early Roman workbenches were built like a Windsor chair. Stout legs were tenoned into a massive top and wedged in place. Traditional French workbenches had massive tops (6" thick), with legs that were big enough to be called tree trunks. Later workbenches relied more on engineering than mass. The classic Continental-style workbench uses a trestle design and dovetails in the aprons and vises to create a bench for the ages. The 19th-century English workbench uses an early torsion-box design to create a stable place to work. And good-quality modern workbenches use threaded rods and bolts to tighten up a design that lacks mass.

Many inexpensive commercial benches are ridiculously rickety. They sway and rack under hand pressure. You can push them across your shop by performing simple operations: routing, sawing, planing. If the bench looks delicate or its components are sized like a modern dining table, I would take a closer look before committing.

Heavy bench. This French-style workbench weighs more than 325 pounds. The top is 4" thick. The legs are 5" square. All this mass absorbs vibration and makes every cutting operation smoother.

A big, thick top and stout legs add mass that will help your work. Heavy cabinet saws with lots of cast iron tend to run smoother. The same goes with benches. Once your bench hits about 300 pounds, it won't move unless you want it to move.

Rule No. 2: Use Stout Joints

Overbuild your workbench by using the best joints. These are times to whip out the through-tenon and dovetail.

If you followed rule no. 1, then rule no. 2 should be no problem. Your joints will be sized to fit the massive scale of your components. If you cannot rely on mass, then you should beef things up with superior joinery. While dovetails and through-tenons are overkill for a towel rack, they are good for a bench.

That's because you are applying racking force to the workbench with typical operations and your vises will do their best to tear apart your bench. All wooden vises need to be overbuilt or they will self-destruct when you

cinch them down hard. I've even seen a vise rip a benchtop from its base.

Make your tenons thick and your mortises deep. If you know how to drawbore a mortise-and-tenon joint, this is one good application. Have you ever been in a timber-framed barn? Did you look at the joints? They're massive and pegged. Imitate that.

I think benches are a good place to practice your skills at cutting these classic joints, but some woodworkers still resist. If that's you, you should investigate hardware to strengthen your bench. Threaded rods, bed bolts, bench bolts, or even stove bolts can turn a spindly assembly into something rigid that can be snugged up if it loosens. The hardware won't give you mass, but it will strengthen a rickety assembly.

Rule No. 3: Pick Wood Based on Stiffness, Not Species

Use a stiff, inexpensive, and common wood to build your bench. Showcase benches made from exotic materials are nice. No argument there; but

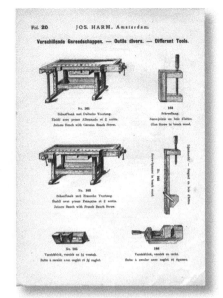

Which wood? These classic European workbenches were made from fine-grained, steamed European beech. Should you do the same? Not necessarily. Choose a wood that is like beech is in Europe: stiff, inexpensive, and plentiful.

Beefy joints. Think big when cutting the joints for your workbench. The small tenons are 1 ¼" thick and 2 ½" long. The larger tenons are 2 ½" thick and 2" long.

Odd workbench designs are nothing new.
This Hammacher, Schlemmer & Co. bench from an old catalog is a study in tool storage. I've seen one of these in person and I can say this: I would not want to have to build anything using it.

focus on the functions before the flash. I'd rather have a construction-lumber bench that followed all these rules than a beautiful European beech bench that skipped even one of these concepts.

There's a lot of confusion on picking a wood for a bench. Most European benches were built using fine-grained, steamed European beech. And many woodworkers go to lengths to purchase precious beech for their workbenches. After all, who wants to argue with hundreds of years of tradition?

I do. European cabinetmakers didn't choose beech because of some magic quality of *Fagus sylvatica*. They chose it because it was dense, stiff, plentiful, and inexpensive. In the United States, beech is dense, stiff, hard to find, and (sometimes) a bit spendy. You can, of course, use it to build a bench, but you will pay a pretty penny for the privilege. And it will have no demonstrable advantage over a cheaper species.

Other woodworkers, tacking toward the sensible, use hard or soft maple for their benches, rationalizing that it is like the beech of the New World. And indeed, the maples have all the qualities of a good species for a workbench.

Maple is stiff, resists denting, and can span long distances without much of a support structure below it. But so can other species. In fact, if you went by the numbers from the wood technologists alone, you'd build your bench from shagbark hickory, despite its difficult nature. Once you look at the characteristics that make a good species for a workbench, you'll see that white oak, southern yellow

pine, fir, or just about any species (excepting basswood and the soft white pines) will perform fine.

Rule No. 4: Use a Tested Design
After you sketch out your workbench design but before you cut any wood, compare your design with historical designs of benches. If your bench appears to be a radical design or looks unlike anything built before, chances are your design is flawed.

I've seen workbenches with pneumatic face vises. Why? I've seen a workbench that had two twin-screw vises: One vise for the right end of the workbench that was matched to work with two long rows of dogs along the length of the benchtop; and a second twin-screw vise on the face of the bench that was matched to two more rows of dogs across the width of the bench.

Now I'm certain that there are a few woodworkers who would really need this arrangement—perhaps someone who has to work on a circular tabletop on one end of the bench and a Windsor chair seat at the other. But for most people who build cabinets and furniture, this setup is redundant and neglects some critical bench functions.

Rule No. 5: Overall Bench Dimensions Are Critical
It is not possible for your bench design to be too heavy or long. But its top can easily be too wide or too tall. I think your benchtop should be as long as possible. Find the wall where your workbench will go (Hint: Pick the wall that has a window). Measure that space. Subtract four feet from that measurement and that's a good

length for the top. Note: The benchtop must be at least 5' long unless you build only small-scale items. Furniture-sized parts typically range up to 48" long and you want to support these fully with a little room to spare.

I've made tops that are 8' long. My next bench will be a 10-footer, the maximum that will fit in my shop. It is difficult to make or imagine a workbench that is too long. The same goes for thickness. It is the thickness that allows the top to be that long. If you make the top really thick (4" or more), then it will offer unerring support and allow you to build your bench without any support system beneath. The top can perch on the legs and will not sag under its own weight.

The width is a different matter. You can have a bench that is too wide for a one-person shop. I've worked on benches that are 36" wide and they have downsides. For starters, if you park them against the wall, you'll have to stretch to reach the tools hanging on the wall. If you assemble projects on your bench, you will find yourself dancing around it a lot more than you should.

But there's more. Cabinetwork is sized in standard chunks. These sizes come from the human body; they aren't arbitrary. A kitchen's base cabinet is generally 24" deep and 34 ½" high. This is important for a couple reasons. First: It means you don't really need a bench that's much more than 24" deep to build cabinets. With that 24" depth, you actually get some advantages, including the fact that you can clamp the cabinet to your bench from as many as three sides of your bench. That's dang handy. A deep bench allows you

to clamp your cabinets to the bench on only two sides (with a couple of exceptions). Here's the other thing to keep in mind: Kitchen cabinets are themselves a highly studied work surface. There's a good reason that kitchen cabinets are 24" deep. And it's the same reason you don't want your workbench much deeper either.

Now I'm not going to argue with you if you build really big stuff or have a bench that you share with another woodworker facing you; you might need more depth. But if you are like the rest of us, a 24"-deep bench is a powerful and right-sized tool.

On the issue of workbench height: Many bench builders worry about it and there are a wide variety of rules and advice. The bottom line is the bench must fit you and your work. And in the end, there are no hard-and-fast rules. I wish there were. Some people like low benches; some like them high.

The right height. Here is how high my workbench is compared to my hand, which is hanging loosely by my side. I use hand and power tools in my work, and I've found this height is ideal.

Nice and long. This early 20th-century airplane factory had the right idea when it came to workbench length. With a long bench, you can work on one end and assemble at the other—no need for an assembly bench. Thus, a big bench actually saves floorspace.

Kitchen Cabinet Door Test. Most benches are easy to set up to work on the faces of boards or assemblies. In this example, a door is clamped between dogs. You can even work simpler and plane against a planing stop.

So consider the following as a good place to start. After taking in my crackpot theories, your next stop should be a friend's house or a wood-working supply store to use their benches and get a feel for what is right (it could be as simple as having a bad back that requires you to have a high bench, or a love for wooden handplanes that dictates a low bench).

Here is my experience with bench height: I started with a bench that was 36" high, which seemed right for someone who is 6' 3 ⅝" tall. And for machine woodworking I was right. The high bench brought the work close to my eyes. I loved it. And then my passion for handwork reared its ugly head.

If you get into hand tools, a high bench becomes less attractive. I started with a jack plane and a few smoothing planes. They worked OK with a high bench, but I became fatigued quickly.

After reading the screed on bench heights, I lowered the height of my 36" bench. It seemed radical, but one day I got the nerve up and sawed 2" off the legs. Those two inches changed my attitude toward planing.

The 34"-bench height allowed me to use my long leg muscles to propel the plane forward instead of my arms.

Now, before you build your next bench at 34" high, stop for a minute. That might not be right for you. Do you use wooden stock planes? If so, you need to consider that the wooden body planes can hold your arms about 3" to 4" higher off the work-bench than a metal plane can. As a result, a wooden plane user's work-bench should be lower.

This is as good reason as ever to get to know someone who has a good shop you can visit and discuss your ideas with. It is better not to make this decision on paper alone.

But there are other factors you must consider when settling on the bench's height. How tall are you? If you are over 6' tall, you should scale your bench a bit higher. Start high and cut it down if it's too high. And prop it up on some blocks of wood if it's too low. Experiment. It's not a highboy; it's a workbench.

Here are other things to consider: Do you work with machinery? If so, a bench that's 34" from the floor—or a bit lower—can be good. The top of a table saw is typically 34" from the floor, so a workbench could be (at most) a great outfeed table or (at least) not in the way of your crosscut-ting and ripping.

Of course, everyone wants a ball-park idea for where to start: Stand up straight and drop your arms against your sides in a relaxed manner. Measure from the floor to the place where your pinky joins your hand. That has been the sweet spot for me.

Rule No. 6: Benches Must Hold the Work in Three Ways

All benches should be able to grip the wood so you can easily work on the faces, the ends, and the edges. Many commercial benches fail on this point.

Submit your bench to what I call the Kitchen Test. Imagine a typical kitchen cabinet door that is ¾" thick, 18" wide, and 24" long. How would you affix that door flat on your bench to level its joints and then sand (or plane) it flat? How would you clamp the door so you could work on the ends to trim the top rail and tops of the stiles so the door will fit its opening? And how will you secure that door on edge so you can rout its hinge mortise and plane off the saw blade marks without the door flopping around? Does your bench pass this test? OK, now ask the same questions with a drawer that is 4" x 18" x 18". And then try a baseboard that is ¾" x 6" x 48".

How you accomplish each of these three functions is up to you and your taste and budget. To work on the faces of boards, you can use a planing stop, a grippy sanding pad, a tail vise with dogs, clamps, or hold-downs.

To work on the ends of boards, you can choose a shoulder vise (especially for dovetailing), a metal quick-release vise, a leg vise, or a twin-screw vise. And you can use all of these in conjunction with a clamp across your bench. The vise holds one corner of the work; the clamp holds the other corner.

Working the long edges of boards is tricky with most benches. In fact, most benches make it difficult to work the edges of long boards, doors or face frames. There are a couple ways to solve this. Older benches had the front edge of the benchtop flush with the front of the legs and stretchers so you could clamp your frames and long boards to the legs. And the older benches also would have a sliding deadman (sometimes called a board jack). It would slide back and forth and had an adjustable peg to support the work from below. Another old form of bench, an English design, had a wide front apron that came down from the top

that was bored with holes for a peg to support long work.

See the sidebar on page 14 for more explanation of viseless workholding.

Rule No. 7: Make Your Bench Friendly to Clamps

Your bench is a three-dimensional clamping surface. Anything that interferes with clamping work to your benchtop (aprons, a drawer bank, doors, supports, etc.) can make some operations a challenge.

There is a trend in workbench design that I personally find troubling. It's a knee-jerk reaction to a common American complaint: We don't think we have enough space in our shops to store our tools and accessories. And how do we solve this problem with our workbenches? By designing them like kitchen cabinets with a countertop work surface.

This design approach gives us lots of drawers below the benchtop, which is great for storing the things you reach for every day. It also can make your bench a pain in the hiney to use for many common operations, such as clamping things to your bench.

Filling up the space below the benchtop also prohibits you from using any type of holdfast or hold-down that I'm aware of.

If you build drawers below the top, how will you clamp objects to the benchtop to work with them? Typically, the banks of drawers below the benchtop prohibit a typical F-style clamp from sneaking in there and lending a hand with the setup. So you can't use a typical clamp to affix a router template to the bench. There are ways around these problems (a

Board ends. Working on the ends of boards—especially wide ones—can be a challenge for face vises. Adding a clamp to the setup stabilizes the work.

Clamping problems. The drawers will interfere with clamping things down to the bench. With no dogs or tail vise, this bench could be frustrating to work on.

Simple long edge work. This primitive bench still allows you to work on long edges of boards. The crochet (or hook) grips the board. Holdfasts and a scrap support from below. Simple and brilliant.

tail vise comes to mind) but the tail vise can be a challenge to install, set, and use.

You can try to cheat (as I have) and install the drawer bank so there is a substantial space underneath the benchtop for holdfasts and clamps. Or you can give your bench a large overhang to allow clamping (as some Shaker-style workbenches did), but then you have to start engineering a way to hold long boards and assemblies on edge.

Rule No. 8: Vise Placement on Your Bench Is Important

Place your vises so they work with your tools. Vises confuse many workbench builders. They're bewildering if you've never spent much time working at a bench to develop a taste for the peccadilloes of all the idiosyncratic forms. There are a lot of weird configurations in the world, from a table with no vises to the bench with a vise on every corner.

Classic workbenches have some sort of vise at the front left corner of

VISELESS WORKHOLDING

You have probably used benches with vises your entire woodworking career. A face vise and tail vise are pretty much the way to go, right? Maybe. Maybe not.

Once you get the hang of it, viseless workholding becomes very fast and can be liberating and fun. Many of these techniques are quite useful, even if you have a vise on your bench.

I find them useful for the entry-level person on a budget as well as for the seasoned woodworker seeking to expand his or her options.

Let's look at how to accomplish some of the more common tasks at a bench: planing faces, edges and ends of boards; crosscutting and ripping; and sawing a couple of joints.

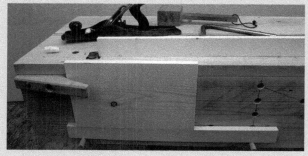

Face planing. Face planing is accomplished by using a planing stop in combination with either battens or a doe's foot (see p. 172). A holdfast keeps the doe's foot in place at the corner of the workpiece to push it against a toothed planing stop. The wedge under the workpiece corner keeps a high corner from rocking. Plane toward your stop and the battens, and don't drag your plane on the return stroke, or the board will pull away from the stop. Flip the doe's foot over if the angle is wrong for a holdfast hole.

Edge planing. Here are two positions for edge planing: One board is in the crochet and supported by pegs (in holes in the apron) and a batten; the other is supported by the benchtop and held against the planing stop. If the pegs are too far apart, place a batten on the pegs and place the edge of your stock upon that. If the workpiece is narrow and flexes under the plane, or doesn't reach above the benchtop with the pegs in their highest position, plane the board against the planing stop on the benchtop. If there are hollows under the board, place wedges in them to keep the board from flexing away from the plane. If the board tips over, you are not planing with even pressure. End grain can be planed in the same manner, but to avoid splintering, plane almost to the corner, then flip the workpiece and finish planing.

the bench. This is called the face vise. Why is it at the left? When we work with hand tools, especially planes, right-handers work from right to left. So having the vise at the left end of the bench is handy because you will always be planing into the vise that is gripping your work, and the work can be braced against the screws of the vise. So if you are a lefty, placing your vise on the front right corner makes sense.

So with that left corner occupied by a vise, where are you going to put the a second vise that is designed to grip boards so you can work on their faces? (The classic vise for this is a tail vise.) Well, the right side of the bench is free (for right-handers) and there is no disadvantage to placing it there, so that's where it generally goes.

Messing with this arrangement can be trouble. I've seen face vises on the right corner of the bench of people who are right-handed. They said they liked it better for crosscutting with a handsaw. But when and if you start handplaning, that vise will be in the way because it won't be ideal for gripping long stock. It will be holding the tail end of the board and the plane will be trying to pull it out of the vise.

Rule No. 9: No Fancy Finishes

When finishing a workbench, less is more. A shiny film finish allows your work to scoot all over the bench. And a film finish will crack when struck by a hammer or dead-blow mallet. Choose a finish that is easy to apply, offers some protection, and doesn't

End grain. A bench hook (see p. 178) can be used as a simple shooting board for longer or wider boards; the plane rides on the benchtop.

Dovetail chopping. Stacking the parts to be chopped saves the need to reset the holdfast individually for each workpiece.

Tenons. Tenoning can be accomplished with the material in the crochet, angled against a peg and held with a holdfast. Angle the board away from you and saw the corners, reverse the board to saw the opposite corners, then cut square across the bottom. Cut the shoulders in the bench hook (or at the end of the bench using pegs and a holdfast).

Dovetail saw cuts. Secure the workpiece against the apron with a thick batten held flush to the benchtop with two holdfasts, and supported by two pegs in the apron's holdfast holes. I like to take a scrap of stock the same thickness as the material being dovetailed and put it to one edge of the chop. I place my holdfast just to the inside of the scrap and give it a good whack. This will keep that end of the chop fixed so that I need only to loosen the other holdfast when changing out parts to be worked.

Finish up. An oil-varnish blend (any brand) is an ideal finish for a workbench. It resists stains, doesn't build up a film, and is easy to apply. Two coats are all I ever use.

Portable. You do need to be able to pull your bench away from the wall on occasion. When I am assembling cabinets, I'll clamp them to the benchtop so I'm able to get around the bench. The same goes when I'm routing. Note how I'm harnessing the window light.

Against the wall. This way, you have the wall and the mass of your bench holding things steady as you saw your workpieces. You also can keep your tools at arm's length. And, the windows cast a useful light on your workbench.

build up a thick film. I like an oil/varnish blend (sold as Danish oil), or just boiled linseed oil.

Rule No. 10: Get a Window Seat

Try to place your bench against a wall and under a window, especially if you use hand tools. The wall braces the workbench as you are planing cross-grain and sawing. The light from the window points out the flaws in the work that your hand tools are trying to remove. (When I work with hand tools, I turn the overhead lights off. I can see much better with fewer light sources.)

For machine work, I find that placing the bench by a window helps with some operations, though not all. When power sanding, for example, the raking window light points out scratches better than overhead fluorescents.

In general, when working with power tools, I tend to pull my workbench away from the wall so I can work on all sides of it. When working with routers, you sometimes have to work with odd clamping setups so that you can rout around a template. So having access to all four sides of the bench is handy. Power tool setups thrive on overhead light—and lots of it. So being by the window is nice, but not as necessary.

HOW TO FIX YOUR CURRENT BENCH

You don't have to build or buy a new workbench if you're frustrated with the one you have. There are ways to improve your bench so it will be more useful. Here are some strategies.

Problem No. 1: My bench is too lightweight. I chase it around the shop when working.
Add weight by building a tray below the bench and fill it with sand. Or rebuild your bench base with massive components and joints. You also can build drawers near the floor (so they don't impede clamping things to the top). That adds weight and storage.

Problem No. 2: My bench sways and vibrates when I work, turning my saw cuts and attempts at planing into a ragged mess.
Your problem is most likely in the bench base. Commercial benches can be too spindly for woodworking. Rebuild the base from massive components and better joints. If you can't do that, stiffen the bench by running all-thread rod through the legs and cinching the base tight with nuts.

Problem No. 3: I want a new bench, but I'm low on funds.
Build your bench using southern yellow pine or fir, both of which are stiff, plentiful, and cheap. You will have to pick your lumber with care and let it reach equilibrium with your shop. But in the end, you'll have a great bench.

Problem No. 4: I think I want a fancy twin-screw vise, Emmert patternmaker's vise, or tail vise on my bench. Plus something for working metal.
Before you drop serious coin on vises and put them on every corner, start with a simple face vise. Then buy a tail vise. Then decide after a year of working on the bench if you need the fancier vises. The answer might be yes. You also might forget that you ever wanted those vises.

Problem No. 5: My bench is too short in length/too wide/narrow/high/low.
If your bench is too short in length, you should probably build a new top. Keep the base if you can. If it's too wide, rip it down (removing a tool tray will help). You might need to cut the base a bit narrower as well. This is doable: Cut the stretchers on the sides shorter and then cut tenons on their ends. Cut new mortises on the legs and assemble it. If your bench is too narrow, scab on new material at the back, which will add mass as well. If your bench is too high, cut down the legs or the sled foot. If it's too low, build a sled foot to raise it.

Problem No. 6: My bench makes it difficult to work on the long edges of boards.
First, detach the benchtop from its base and reattach it so the legs are flush with the front edge of the benchtop. If your bench has a sled foot or a trestle design, there is an easier fix. Scab on extra pieces to the legs to bring them flush with the front of the benchtop. Now build a sliding deadman or a bench slave and you'll be in business.

Problem No. 7: My bench looks like a kitchen counter with drawers below. Clamping to the bench is a problem.
You might be stuck here. Some commercial designs allow you to remove the drawer bank (they sell them separately) and you can install it someplace else handy, such as under a table saw's wing. If your bench is a door on top of base cabinets, consider making a new base and use that cabinet as a cabinet.

Problem No. 8: My commercial bench came with face and tail vises. Both rack horribly.
Throw them in the fireplace and install a real face vise on the front and tail vise on the end.

Problem No. 9: My workbench has a lacquer finish that looks nasty and lets the work slide everywhere.
Flatten the top of your workbench and then refinish the top with an oil/varnish blend.

Problem No. 10: I like my bench in the middle of the room so I can work on all sides.
Perhaps you do. Try putting it under a window and against the wall and work that way for a few months. Don't have a window? Directional compact florescent fixtures can help. Or you can save your pennies and have a window installed. I did. It was the best money I've ever spent on my shop.

   A well-designed, solidly built, and properly outfitted bench is the most useful tool in the workshop. Anything less is only making you struggle. ■

THE 24-HOUR WORKBENCH

This workbench is sturdy, inexpensive, and doesn't take a month of Sundays to build.

BY CHRISTOPHER SCHWARZ & KARA GEBHART

Whenever we leave beginning woodworkers to work alone in the shop, it's a fair bet that when we return to check on them, they're working on the shop's floor.

We have at least five workbenches in our shop—not counting the assembly tables—but the new people always seem to prefer the wide expanse of the concrete floor more than the benches. Of course, I shouldn't talk. When I started woodworking I had my grandfather's fully outfitted bench. But my first few projects were built on the floor of our back porch, my assemblies propped up on a couple of 4x4s. I can't for the life of me remember why I chose the floor instead of the bench.

Since those early years, I've built a few workbenches. And I've been striving to make each one more versatile, solid, inexpensive, and quick to build than the last. I think I've finally got it. To test my theory, Associate Editor Kara Gebhart and I built this bench with a shoestring budget and just 24 hours of working shop time. And that 24 hours includes everything, even the two hours we spent picking out the wood and sawing it to rough length on a dolly in the parking lot of the lumberyard. (But once again, I was working on the ground. Oh, drat.)

The real beauty of this bench (besides getting you off the floor) is that it can be completed using tools you likely already have in your shop.

For this project, your must-have tools are a table saw, a drill press, a corded drill, and some basic hand tools. If you have a jointer and planer, the project will go faster because you can easily dress your lumber to size and eliminate any bowing or warping. But don't be afraid to work with the lumber as it comes from the lumberyard. Just make sure you buy the straightest pieces you can.

START WITH THE ROUGH STUFF
TIME: 0:00 to 5:06
In a nutshell, here's how the bench goes together: The top is made of four

pieces of Baltic birch plywood that are laminated together with a pine "skirt" glued around the edge. On the bench's pine base, the end rails are joined to the legs using pegged mortise-and-tenon joints. The end assemblies attach to the front and back rails using an unglued mortise-and-tenon joint with big bench bolts—it's quite similar to a bed in construction.

When we first went to the lumberyard, it seemed like a good idea to buy 4x4 posts for the legs. But when we got there (and later called around to other nearby lumberyards) we discovered that the only 4x4s available in yellow pine were #2 common, which has more knots than the #1 pine (also sold as "prime" or "top choice" in some yards). If you can't get yellow pine where you live, you can just look for fir.

After picking through the mound of knotty 4x4s, we decided to instead make the legs by ripping a 2x8 and gluing up the legs to the thickness that we needed. It took longer to

BENCH OPTIONS

The beauty of this bench is that it can be used as a standalone workbench or as an outfeed table for your table saw. At 34" high, this bench is the same height as most cabinet saws on the market. And if you make the legs ½" longer, the bench will be at the height of most contractor saws (check yours before you begin).

If you want a toolbox for this bench, see page 100. The toolbox under the Power Tool Workbench is designed to fit perfectly under this bench, too. And the toolbox is built using one 4' x 8' sheet of ¾" plywood and one sheet of ½" plywood.

make the legs this way, but now they have almost no knots.

Crosscut and rip the parts you need for the base of the bench and the skirt that goes around the top. If you have a planer and jointer, dress your lumber. Now glue up and clamp the parts for the legs and get out your clamp collection and some buckets (yes, buckets) to glue up the top.

TOP-DOWN CONSTRUCTION
TIME: 5:06 to 6:29

I've built a few of these and have come up with an easy way to make the top: Sandwich all the plywood into a nearly 3"-thick slab. We glued it up one layer at a time to keep things under control and to ensure we could eliminate all gaps on the edges.

Clamps aplenty. Use whatever clamps are on hand to glue the top together. If you're low on clamps, you can use 5-gallon buckets of water (they are quite heavy) in the middle, the four cauls discussed, and C-clamps along the edges.

You're probably going to need at least four 8-ounce bottles of yellow glue for this part of the project, plus a scrap of plywood (¼" x 4" x 7" worked for us) to spread the glue evenly. Squirt a sizable amount onto one piece of plywood and spread the adhesive until you've got a thin and even film. Place the plywood's mating piece on top and line up the edges. Now drive about a dozen #8 x 1¼" screws into the two pieces. Space the screws evenly across the face of the board, but you don't need to get scientific about it. The object is to pull the two pieces together without gaps. After 30 minutes of drying time, remove the screws and add another layer of glue, plywood and some more screws.

Because you don't want a bunch of screw holes staring at you every time you use the bench, you'll likely want to attach the final layer with clamps, clamping cauls, and anything else heavy you have in your shop.

We used four cauls (a clamping aid) across the width of the top to put even more pressure in the middle. The cauls should be about 2" x 2" x 32". Plane or sand a ¹⁄₁₆" taper toward each end to give each caul a slight bow. When you clamp the bow against the top, this will put pressure in the middle of your slab.

Finally, use whatever other clamps you have to clamp the edges (C-clamps work well).

When all four layers are glued together, cut your top to its finished size using a circular saw and a straight scrap of wood to guide it. Because the top is so thick, you'll have to cut from both faces, so lay out cutting lines with care.

SKIRT WILL TEST YOUR SKILLS
TIME: 6:29 to 11:49

Now gather the skirt pieces and begin laying out the finger joints for the corners. These joints are mostly decorative. Butt joints or miters will do just as well (and save you some time). And if you want to make this process even easier, use ½"-thick material for the skirt, which is a whole lot easier to clamp in place because it is more flexible than some of the thicker material.

Here's how we suggest you cut the finger joints: First lay out the joints on the end pieces with just one tongue or finger sticking out. Each finger is 1 ⅜" long and 1" wide. Cut the waste away using a handsaw or bandsaw and check the fit against your top. When it fits perfectly, use these joints to lay out the mating joints on the long skirt pieces. Cut the notches

on the long skirt pieces and check the fit of your joints. Tune them up using a chisel, a rabbet plane, or a shoulder plane.

Now glue the skirt pieces to the top. Because each ply in plywood runs the opposite direction of the ply above it, there's actually a fair amount of long grain on the edges of

Skirt joinery. The skirt pieces can be joined using finger joints, a miter, or just wood screws. If you choose finger joints, your best bet is to lay out and cut the joint on one member and then use that joint to lay out your cut lines on its mate.

CUT LIST & MATERIALS

	NO.	ITEM	DIMENSIONS (INCHES)			MATERIAL	COMMENTS
			T	W	L		
☐	1	Top*	3	24 ¼	58 ¼	Baltic birch plywood	
☐	2	Top skirt, ends	1 ⅜	3	27	Southern yellow pine	
☐	2	Top skirt, front and back	1 ⅜	3	61	Southern yellow pine	
☐	4	Legs	3	3	31	Southern yellow pine	
☐	4	End rails	1 ⅜	3	23 ½	Southern yellow pine	2" TBE†
☐	2	Front and back rails	1 ⅜	7	40	Southern yellow pine	¾" TBE
☐		Joint pegs	⅜ dia		2 ⅛	Dowel	
☐	1	Large front vise with 1 ⅛" dia. screw		10 ½	21		13" clamping capacity
☐	1	Vise handle	1 ⅛ dia.				
☐	1	Vise jaw	2 ¾	6	15	Southern yellow pine	
☐	4	Bench bolts	⅝ dia.		6		
☐	4	Corner braces		5	5		
☐		Dog pegs	¾ dia		3	Dowel	
☐		Dog faces	⅝	1 ½	1 ½	Scrap	

* The top is laminated using four layers of ¾"-thick Baltic birch plywood. † TBE = Tenon both ends.

your top. This means the skirt will stay stuck just fine using only glue. Add as many clamps as you can. While that glue dries, start reading the directions for installing the vise, because that's the next step.

Before you begin, be sure your drill press's table is square to the chuck—this will save you lots of frustration. Once you get your vise installed, place the top on a couple of sawhorses (you'll need a friend's help) and get ready to build the base.

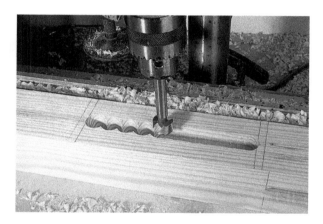

Clean mortises. Use your drill press to first drill a series of overlapping holes. Then go back and clean up the waste between these holes several times until the bit can slide left to right in the mortise without stopping. Then you only have to square up the ends with a chisel.

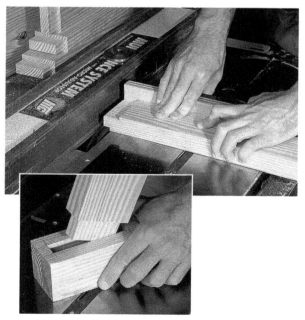

Dado stack. This method requires only one saw setup to make all the cuts on a tenon. First define the tenon's face cheeks and shoulders (right). Then you can define the edge cheeks and shoulders. Finally, check your work using the test mortise you cut earlier (bottom).

A STOUT BASE
TIME: 11:49 to 14:54

The base of this bench is built with mortise-and-tenon joints. The two assembled ends are glued together and then pegged using dowels. The ends are attached to the front and back rails using an unglued mortise-and-tenon joint plus bench bolts.

The first step is to make a practice mortise in a piece of scrap that you can use to size all your tenons. We made our mortises on a drill press using a ¾"-diameter Forstner bit and a fence. You can make really clean mortises this way. After you've made your test mortise, head to the table saw to make all of your tenons.

I make my tenons using a dado stack in my table saw. The fence determines the length of the tenon; the height of the dado blades determines the measurement of the tenons' shoulders. Set the height of the dado stack to ⁵⁄₁₆", cut a tenon on some scrap as shown in the photos, and see if it fits your test mortise. If the fit is firm and smooth, cut all the tenons on the front, back, and end rails.

Use your tenons to lay out the locations of your mortises on the legs. Use the diagrams as a guide. Cut mortises using your drill press and get ready to install the bench bolts.

BIG BAD BENCH BOLTS
TIME: 14:54 to 18:59

Don't get the cheapest set of bench bolts for this project, or it will be tough to put everything together.

You can begin installing the bench bolts by drilling a 1⅛"-diameter x ½"-deep counterbore in the legs that's centered on the location of the rail. Then drill a ⅝"-diameter hole in the center of that counterbore that goes all the way through the leg into the mortise you cut earlier.

Now dry-assemble the ends plus the front and back rails and clamp everything together. Use a 5/8" brad-point drill bit to mark the center of your hole on the end of each tenon.

Disassemble the bench and clamp the front rail to your top or in a vise. Use a doweling jig and a 5/8" drill bit to continue boring the hole for the bench bolt. You'll need to drill about 3 3/4" into the rail. Then repeat this process on the other tenons.

Now you need to drill a 1 1/4"-diameter hole that intersects the 5/8" hole you just drilled in the rail. This 1 1/4"-diameter hole holds a special round nut that pulls everything together. To accurately locate where this 1 1/4" hole should be, I made a simple jig (see below) I picked up from another project. This works like a charm and I recommend you use one. Sometimes drill bits can wander— even when guided by a doweling jig— and this simple jig ensures success.

Plane or sand all your legs and rails, then assemble the bench's base. First, glue the end rails between the

Mark the counterbore. Once you've drilled the counterbore and the through-hole for the bench bolt, mark its location on the end of the tenon using a brad-point bit.

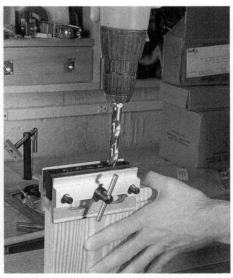

Bench bolt hole. Drill a hole for the bench bolt using a doweling jig and a 5/8"-diameter drill bit. It's a deep hole, so you might need an extra-long bit to do the job.

legs. Glue and clamp that assembly. When it's dry, drill a 3/8"-diameter hole through each joint that's about 2" deep. Then glue and hammer a peg through the tenons using 2 1/8"-long sections of 3/8"-diameter dowel stock into each hole. Then install the bench bolts and use a ratchet and socket to snug your bolts and bring everything together.

Simple jig. To accurately position the hole for the brass nut, build a simple jig like the one shown here using 5/8" dowel, a scrap of wood, and a nail. The nail is located where you want the center of the brass nut to go (left). Insert the dowel into the hole in the rail and tap the nail (right). Then just drill a 1 1/4"-diameter hole there and your joint will go together with ease.

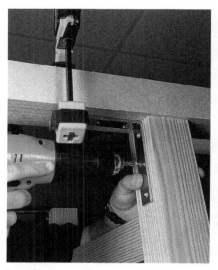

Install brackets. Secure the top to the base with this simple trick. Lay a scrap board across the legs and clamp the bracket to it. Now screw the bracket to the leg.

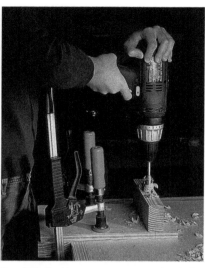

Dog-hole jig. Here you can see our dog-hole drilling jig in action. There are two ¾" holes in the plywood base: one for the bit and the other to allow us to see the layout marks on the benchtop.

Now screw the 5" braces to the legs using the photo on at left as a guide. Turn the top upside down on the saw-horses and place the assembled base in position. Screw it down.

DOG HOLES AND DETAILS
TIME: 18:59 to 23:02

Dog holes on a bench are essential for clamping large panels, holding table legs, and even clamping difficult-to-clamp assemblies. Most round dog holes are ¾" in diameter so they accept a wide range of commercial dogs.

We made our own dogs for this bench to keep us from blowing our budget. Our homemade dogs are made using 3"-long sections of ¾" dowel screwed to ⅝" x 1½" x 1½" pieces of scrap hardwood.

First drill the dog hole in your tail vise's jaw using your drill press. While you have the vise jaw off the bench, go ahead and add the edge detail of your choice to the ends. We chose a traditional large bead. A chamfer would be quicker if you're pressed for time.

Now put the vise's jaw back on and lay out the locations of your dog holes in the top. They can be anywhere from 8" to 11" apart. You'll have to build a simple jig to cut the holes. It's made from three pieces of scrap and is shown in action in the photo at top right.

We bored the dog holes using a ¾" auger bit in a corded drill. Use a low speed on your drill for this operation because you need buckets of torque.

Chamfer the rim of each dog hole; this prevents the grain from ripping up when you pull the occasionally stubborn dog from its hole (bad dog!).

BENCH BOLT JOINT

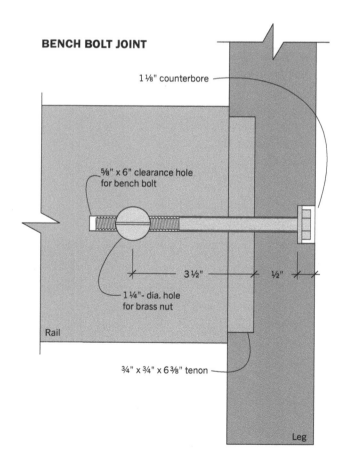

1 ⅛" counterbore

⅝" x 6" clearance hole for bench bolt

1 ¼"- dia. hole for brass nut

3½"

½"

¾" x ¾" x 6 ⅜" tenon

Rail

Leg

You can just use a chamfer bit in your plunge router to make this cut. Or you can simply ease the rims using some coarse sandpaper.

We sanded the top by using 120-grit sandpaper in a random-orbit sander and called it a day. Break all the sharp edges using 120-grit sandpaper. You don't need a fancy finish on this bench—just something to protect it from spills and scrapes. We took some off-the-shelf satin poly-urethane, thinned it down to three parts poly and one part mineral spirits, and ragged on two coats. Allow the finish to dry at least four hours between coats. (No, the four hours of drying time isn't included in our total time.)

Then we turned the stopwatch off and checked our time: 23 hours and 2 minutes. We had just enough time left to sweep the floor. ■

PLAN

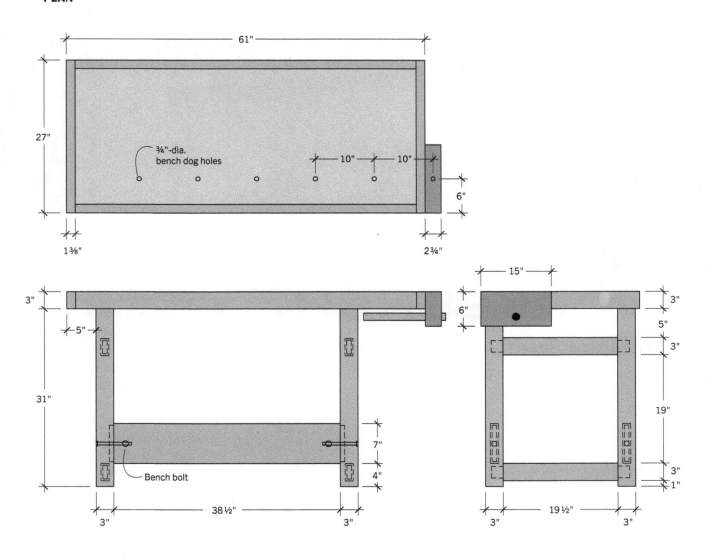

21ST-CENTURY WORKBENCH

This hybrid design holds work any which way you want to.

BY ROBERT W. LANG

Good design is little more than selective thievery. This workbench is a good example of that. A combination of features from several historic forms, ranging from the Roubo to the Workmate, becomes a new form, suited to being the center of a modern woodworking shop. I've never seen a workbench that I was entirely happy with. I have love/hate relationships with many common features. I like tool trays, but hate the way shavings and other detritus collects in them. I want to be able to clamp work quickly, but speed means nothing if the clamping isn't solid and secure. Good design is also the art of compromise, finding the happy medium between extremes.

This bench began with the idea of building a reproduction of an English Nicholson bench. The Nicholson was popular in Colonial America, and variations of it appeared in wood-working books until the 1920s. The dominant feature on the Nicholson is a wide front apron, which allows work to be secured to the front of the bench as well as to the top. The draw-back to the extended apron is that it limits the ability to clamp down to the top of the bench from the edge. I narrowed and lowered the apron so I could clamp work to the bench in two directions. I was also intrigued by the knockdown joinery on some of the historic Nicholson benches.

While I don't plan on moving my bench very often, I decided to make it in manageable chunks, both to ease the process of making it and of assembling it. The design is based on function in the completed bench, and also on the process of making, moving, and maintaining it. The equipment I used to make it are basic home-shop tools—a 10" hybrid table saw, a 6"-inch jointer, and a 12" "lunchbox" planer. And I didn't need a bench to build my bench. I made the top first, then placed that on a pair of horses.

GETTING IT STRAIGHT, ONE PART AT A TIME

The best reason for assembling the top of the bench first is that, when it is complete, it can be put to work to fabricate and assemble all the other parts. It's almost as good as having

TOP VIEW

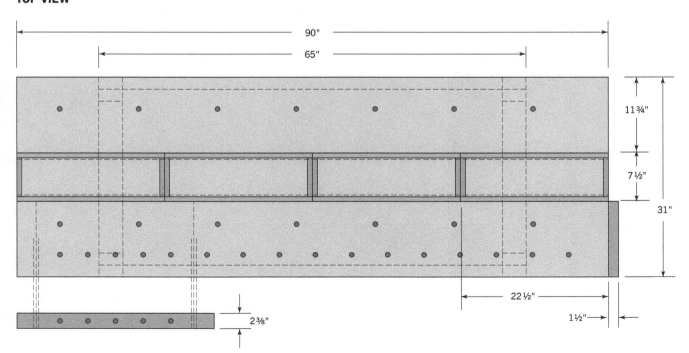

Spread with speed. A disposable paint roller applies an even coat of yellow glue quickly. Apply the glue to one side of the lamination only. Doing both sides wastes time and glue.

a place to sit down when you're halfway through building a chair. I began with rough 8/4 ash lumber, and picked through my stock for the straightest pieces to use for the top. After running one edge over the jointer, I ripped each piece to a rough width of 3 ¼". I then dressed one face of each piece flat on the jointer. When I had 14 pieces ready, I moved to the planer. I wanted the stock to be at least 1 ⅞" thick, but stopped milling when I had two clean faces. Each half of the top consists of six pieces glued face-to-face, and leaving the parts as thick as possible allowed me to maximize the width. If the stock had ended up thinner than planned, I would have added a seventh piece. The goal was to have the halves of the top finish at least 11 ½" wide, but less than 12".

FRONT VIEW

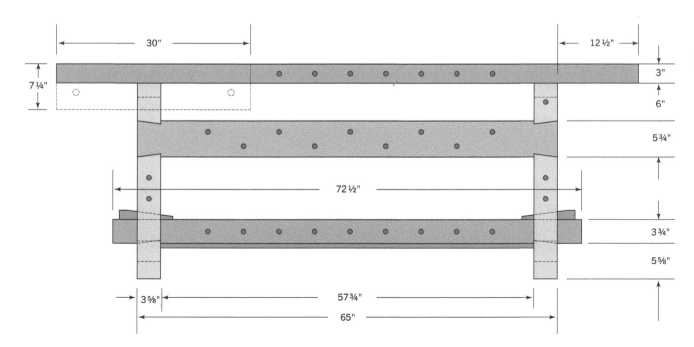

The length of the bench was also a variable. I wanted a minimum length of 84", but I was able to get clean lengths of 90" from the 8'-long rough material. After all the parts were milled, I let them sit over a weekend to be sure the wood wasn't going to move or warp. I began laminating the top boards in pairs glued face-to-face. To keep them flat, I clamped them together on the strongest, straightest surface available: an I-beam made of ¾"-thick plywood. I let each pair sit in the clamps for at least four hours, and then for another 24 hours to allow the glue to dry.

BACK TO MILLING, THEN SERIOUS GLUING

I ran the edges of each glued pair over the jointer to get a straight, square edge on each lamination. I then ran the boards on edge through the planer. Once again, I stopped when I had two clean surfaces rather than taking the boards to a specific thickness. The cleaned-up pairs were slightly over my planned 3" thickness, but I would still need to remove some material after gluing up each top section. How much to remove would depend on how well these pieces went together.

I set two long boards between my horses, and placed square boards across them, about a foot apart. This gave me a nice level surface to work on, and provided the ability to reach around, over, or under the tops as I was setting the clamps. A test-stacking of three pairs of boards gave me the confidence to glue each half-top section in one go. With nearly every clamp in the shop standing by, I spread yellow glue on one face

Sum of its parts. The flatness of the finished benchtop depends on the quality of its component parts. Milling the pieces as true as possible and gluing them together on a flat surface is crucial.

Practice makes perfect. Taking time to set up a level and accessible surface for gluing, and making a dry run, makes the final glue-up stress-free and yields good results.

Power lunch. This bench was designed around available machinery. After cleaning one surface with a handplane, the opposite surface is planed on a portable machine.

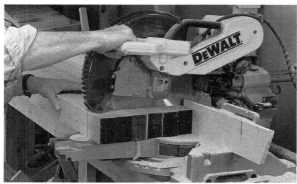

It just fits. Trimming the top halves to final length is within the capacity of this 12" sliding compound miter saw.

of two of the parts with a 3"-wide paint roller. With an even coat of glue applied, I turned the parts 90° and starting tightening the clamps, working from the center out to the ends. Wooden hand screws across the ends of the glue joints prevented the parts from sliding out of place. I removed any glue squeeze-out with a wet rag and a scraper, and let the pieces sit in the clamps overnight.

Because I had carefully milled the parts before gluing, and glued carefully on a flat surface, the tops were in good shape coming out of the clamps. I knocked down the high spots with a handplane to get a flat surface, and ran the assembled tops through the portable thickness planer. Leaving the top halves less than 12" wide allowed me to use this small machine for surfacing. At some

DETAIL: LEG

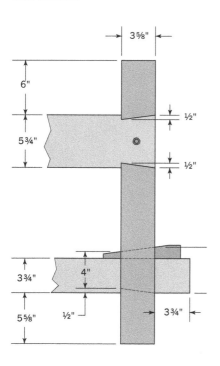

SIDE VIEW

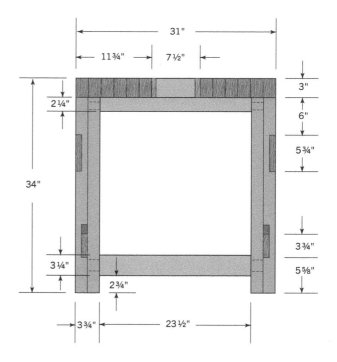

point in the future, I may need to resurface the top, and the little planer will always be an option. This strategy also allowed me to cut each top half to length with my sliding compound miter saw.

THE STRUCTURE DOWN BELOW

Joinery on a bench is on a different scale than joinery for furniture. The parts are larger, and the emphasis is more on function and strength than appearance. The legs are two pieces glued face-to-face, and each pair of legs is connected with an upper and a lower stretcher with mortise-and-tenon joints. The legs and stretchers are assembled into units, and the two ends are connected with rails running the length of the bench. The large scale of the components made it possible to locate joints for the knockdown connections in the outer halves of the legs, and these joints were cut before the legs were laminated together.

In furniture, I use through-tenons to show off; in this bench, I used them to make life easier. The mortises are only cut in the inner half of each leg. After laying out the joints, I removed most of the waste at the drill press with a ¾"-diameter Forstner bit. Working on my new benchtops placed on horses, I used a chisel to square the mortises to the layout lines. I then cut the tenons to fit the mortises. I cut most of the shoulders by hand, but also cut some on the table saw to compare techniques. The hand-cut shoulders were a bit neater, and didn't take much longer to make. After cutting the shoulders, I removed the waste around the tenons at the table saw, using the miter

Minimize the layout. After laying out the tenon locations on the stretchers, lines are transferred to mark the matching mortises on the inner parts of the legs.

Wasting away. A ¾" Forstner bit in the drill press is used to remove most of the material from the through-mortises in the inner legs.

Chop for an easy fit. A bit of chisel work cleans up the mortises to the layout lines at top and bottom. Widening the sides allows an easier fit and stronger joint with the addition of wedges.

Tenons, plan B.
The tenons can also be cut on the table saw, but the machine must be adjusted several times to hit the layout lines precisely.

Shoulders by hand.
I think it's faster to cut the shoulders by hand and avoid exacting setups on a machine. It's just a matter of cutting to the lines.

Together forever.
After assembling the leg and stretcher joints, wedges are glued and driven in the joint from the outside to lock it permanently.

gauge to guide the boards across a stack-dado set. With a shoulder plane and rasp, I fine-tuned the fit of the joints. After tweaking a couple to a perfect fit, I realized I could make the tenons narrow in width, widen the outside of the mortises with a quick chisel cut, then secure the joints from outside with wedges. This saved time and gave stronger joints. With the tenons wedged, they can't pull out of the mortises. After letting the glue dry, I trimmed the wedges with a flush-cutting saw, followed by a block plane.

GREAT BIG DOVETAILS

It's easy to think of dovetails as decorative joints, but there are many practical reasons for using this joint to hold the ends of the bench together. Most of the stress on a bench in use is end to end, and the wedged shape of the rail-to-leg joints can't be pulled apart. In fact, if you push the base of this bench from the end, the joints tighten rather than loosen. The dovetails also serve to positively locate and align the parts during final assembly. As the joints come together, they fit where they fit; it isn't possible to put them together in the wrong place.

Both upper and lower dovetail joints are half-lapped with the outer portion of the leg. The lower joint is on the inside of the leg and is a half dovetail; the other half of the joint is a removable wedge. The upper joint is on the outside of the leg and secured by a lag bolt. After cutting the shoulders by hand, I removed the waste with the dado stack on the table saw, and used a roller stand to support the long workpieces. The angled cuts were made with a jigsaw. I smoothed out the waste left by the dado cutters with a chisel, shoulder plane, and rasp, then marked the locations of the sockets on the outer legs directly from the tails. I cut the angled ends of the sockets with a backsaw, and removed most of the waste in between at the table saw. The remaining waste was removed with a chisel, followed by a shoulder plane. Then I used a plane maker's float to achieve a flat bottom on these joints.

The upper joints need to be equal in thickness so that the outer surfaces of the legs and rails will be flush when the bench is assembled. Down at the lower rail, the tail needs to be thinner than the socket so that the end of the rail can easily pass through the socket in the leg. The socket also needs to be wide enough to allow the square end of the rail to enter the narrow portion of the joint, then drop down into place. This requires some fussing, but because the outer half of the leg is loose at this point, it's easy to see what is going on while adjusting the joint. After fitting the lower portion of the tail, I cut

and fit the removable wedges. With the joinery complete, I spread glue on the inside surface, and glued the outer legs to the previously assembled inner legs and stretchers, taking care to keep the parts aligned. After letting the glue dry overnight, I was anxious to see the completed bench.

Halfway gone. The dovetails on the ends of the horizontal rails are half-lapped. I removed most of the material with a dado stack set on the table saw. An adjustable roller stand supported the other end of the long parts.

Real-time layout. After making the male part of the joint, the socket is laid out directly from the finished part. Simply lay the rail in position, line up the top, and knife in the angled line.

Fit the joint, then the wedge. After fitting the dovetail for the lower rail, a matching wedge is cut and fit. Thanks to working on only half the leg, this process is entirely visible.

A little skinny. The end of the rail will need to easily pass through the assembled leg. The square is set to half the thickness, and the space below the blade tells the story.

SCREWS, WEDGES, AND THE HOLE STORY

I set the completed end units on the floor, inserted the two lower rails into one end, knocked in the wedges, then slid the rails into the other end. The upper rails were knocked into place, and after marking the centers of the tails, I made a ¾"-diameter counter-bore deep enough to leave the head of a lag screw ⅛" below the surface.

Then I drilled a pilot hole and drove in a ¼" x 2" lag screw. I set the tops in place on the assembled base, with the edges even with the outside of the legs and a consistent distance in between. I drilled ⅜"-diameter through holes in the upper stretchers, and ¼"-diameter pilot holes in the bottom surface of the tops. Four ⁵⁄₁₆" x 3 ½" lag screws secure each top section to the base.

After admiring the assembly for a while, I laid the bench on its side and flushed the joints to each other. The front of the bench is really a working work-holding surface, so I took care to level all the parts to be in the same plane. While I was at it, I used my block plane to bring the ends of the tails even with the edges of the legs.

Setting the bench back on its feet, I laid out the locations of the vises, as well as the ¾"-diameter holes in the top, front rails, and front legs. A twin-screw vise straddles the left-front leg, and a small quick-release vise is in the tail-vise position. I routed out a recess in the end of the benchtop for the tail vise, and glued two 2"-thick x 4 ¼"-wide blocks to the bottom to hold the screws for the larger twin-screw vise.

Careful now. The legs are permanently assembled by gluing. Judicious placement of glue to keep it out of the joint, and a clamp across the bottom to keep the parts from sliding, make the process painless.

A short side trip. After assembling the rails and top halves, the bench is turned on its side to level the front surfaces.

There is a line of holes in the top centered on the dog location in the end vise. I drew a line the length of the bench at this distance, then marked a hole to just-miss each side of the right-hand leg. I set a pair of dividers at this distance and stepped off the center-to-center marks for this line of holes.

I carried these marks down to the front rails using a framing square. The holes in the lower rail are centered vertically, and the ones in the upper rail alternate high and low, 1¾" in from the edges. The holes in the rails don't need to line up with the holes in the top, but it seemed a reasonable spacing. It was easier to transfer the existing layout than to think about a new one. The holes in the front will be used with a surface clamp, or a simple dog to support work from below. On the inside edge of the top, I marked out locations for holdfast holes on 12" centers, 3" in from the back edge on the front half. On the back half is another row of holdfast holes, also on 12" centers. I wanted these roughly in the middle of the top, but didn't want to drill into the glue line, so I centered them in the middle of the board beyond the center of the rear top.

There are five holes in the front jaw of the vise aligned with the holes in the top, roughly in the center and near each end of the jaw. Each of the front legs also has holes, two in the left, equally spaced between the upper and lower rails. The holes in the right leg match, with an additional hole in the space between the upper rail and the benchtop.

Because the parts of the bench are relatively manageable components,

Fine-tuning. The lag screws that secure the upper rails are counterbored to keep the heads well below the surface. The faces of the rails are made flush to the legs.

The boring part. The top halves are heavy, but with the aid of a stand they can be brought to the drill press for boring the dog and holdfast holes.

Even ends. The ends of the tails are also trimmed flush. The lag bolts that hold the top on are visible behind the block plane.

I took the bench apart and drilled all of the holes at the drill press using a ¾"-diameter brad-point bit at a low speed: about 500 rpm. I used my roller stand to support the long parts that hung off the drill press table.

WHERE WILL THE HAMSTERS SLEEP?

Between the two lower rails is a shelf that is supported by 2"-wide cleats nailed to the bottom of the rails. The shelf boards are random widths of 4/4 material, with opposing rabbets

EXPLODED VIEW

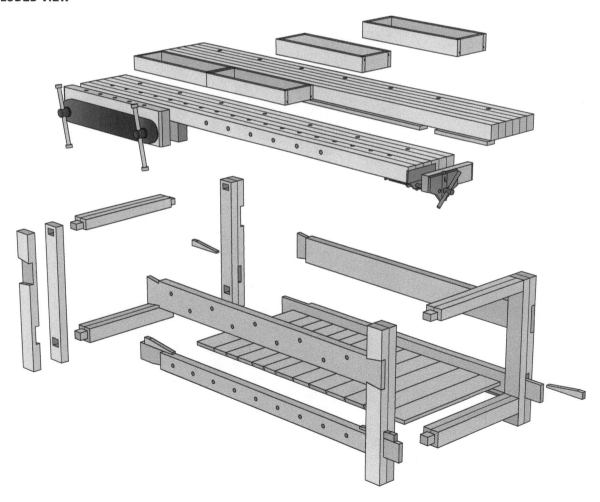

on the long edges. The boards at each end have a rabbet on only one edge, and butt against the inside edge of the lower stretchers. The shelf boards and cleats were left as thick as possible, and cleats were also nailed to the underside of each inside edge of the top sections to support the removable tool trays. The trays are open-topped boxes, made from ¾"-thick solid wood. The corners are held together with simple rabbet-in-groove joints. The bottom is rabbeted

to fit in a ¼"-wide groove, with the face of the bottom even with the bottom edges of the box sides.

The tool trays can be turned upside down if desired to make the entire bench, or just portions of it, one wide flat surface. Or they can be removed to allow clamping to the middle of the benchtop. They can also be easily carried to return tools to their homes, or to the trash can to remove the inevitable accumulation of shavings and other trash.

I don't believe that a bench needs a fine finish. After planing all the surfaces, I knocked off the sharp corners of the edges and applied a coat of Danish oil. With a few holdfasts and hold-downs, along with some F-style clamps, I can hold work securely in almost any position. That's what a good bench is for. It is the tool that makes the work of all the other tools easier and more efficient. ■

CUT LIST & MATERIALS

	NO.	ITEM	DIMENSIONS (INCHES)			MATERIAL	COMMENTS
			T	W	L		
☐	12	Top laminates	1 15/16	3	90	Ash	Mill TAP*, 6 per half
☐	4	Inner legs	1 15/16	3 ¾	31	Ash	Mill TAP, 1 ¾" minimum
☐	4	Outer legs	1 15/16	3 ¾	31	Ash	Mill TAP, 1 ¾" minimum
☐	4	Upper stretchers	1 15/16	2 ¼	31	Ash	Mill TAP, 1 ¾" minimum
☐	4	Lower stretchers	1 15/16	3 ¼	31	Ash	Mill TAP, 1 ¾" minimum
☐	2	Upper rails	1 15/16	6	65	Ash	Mill TAP, 1 ¾" minimum
☐	2	Lower rails	1 15/16	3 ¾	72 ½	Ash	Mill TAP, 1 ¾" minimum
☐	4	Wedges	⅞	1 ⅜	8 ⅝	Ash	Mill TAP, 1 ¾" minimum
☐	4	Cleats	13/16	2	90	Ash	Cut to fit between ends
☐	8	Box sides	¾	3	22 ½	Ash	
☐	8	Box ends	¾	3	6 ¾	Ash	
☐	4	Box bottoms	¾	6 ¾	20 ½	Ash	
☐	1	Shelf	¾	22 ⅜	58	Ash	Random-width shiplapped boards
☐	1	Face vise blocks	2	4 ¼	30	Ash	Total length, trim for each side of leg
☐	1	Face vise chop	2 ⅜	7 ¼	30	Ash	Laminated from 3 pieces
☐	1	Tail vise chop	1 ½	3	11 ¾	Ash	
☐	1	Twin-screw vise, 24" center					
☐	1	Quick-release bench vise			7"		
☐	2	Surface clamp for 3/4" hole					
☐	4	Bench dogs	4 ⅜"-dia.				
☐	4	Holdfasts					
☐	4	Lag screws	¼		2		
☐	4	Lag screws	5/16		3 ½		

* TAP = Thick as possible

MASTER CABINETMAKER'S BENCH

This proven design will last a lifetime.

BY ALAN TURNER

I have many fine tools in my shop, but the most important one is my bench. It has a classic design, favored by cabinetmakers for generations.

I've spent a long time refining the details of this bench. I've built 15 of them over the years, simplifying and improving the design each time. At

Philadelphia Furniture Workshop, where I teach, I've helped students build dozens more.

The materials are top-notch. I've used the best wood (3"-thick hard maple), the best tail vise hardware (imported from Germany), and made the bench plenty big and very heavy (it's 7' long and weighs 250 lbs). The materials aren't cheap, but for a lifetime of service, they're worth every penny.

KEY FEATURES

■ Thick top. It will always stay flat. At 2 ⅝" thick, it won't bend when you plane a board or bounce when you chop mortises.

■ Robust, knockdown base. It will stand stiff under any pressure. It can easily be disassembled or retightened.

■ Strong, versatile vises. You can hold work in nearly any position: between dogs, using the tail vise; vertical or horizontal, using the face vise; perpendicular, again using the

tail vise; and flat—anywhere on the top—using a holdfast.

BUILD THE BASE

Before you begin building, decide what height is best for you. It's easy to make this bench taller by adding thicker pads under the feet, but hard to make it shorter, once it's built.

Be picky about the wood for the entire bench, which is all hard maple. Reject boards that are twisted; they may never stay flat. Machine the

EXPLODED VIEW

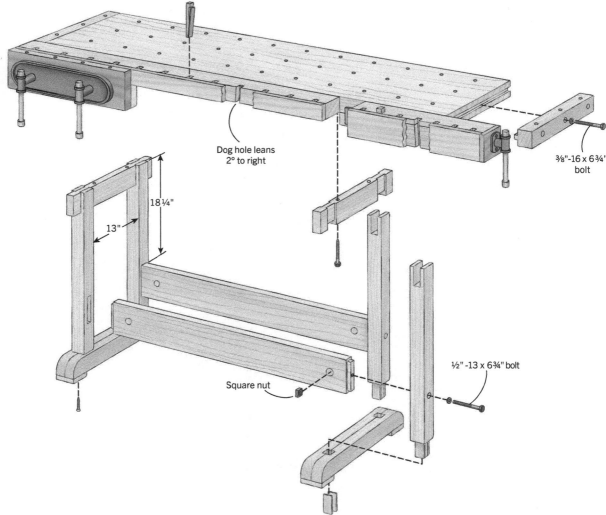

Dog hole leans
2° to right

18¼"

13"

⅜"-16 x 6¾"
bolt

Square nut

½" -13 x 6¾" bolt

EXPLODED VIEW: BASE JOINERY

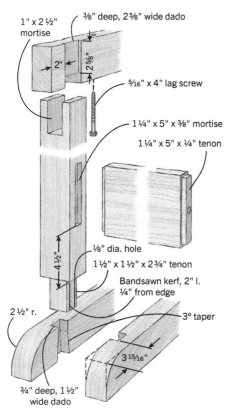

1" x 2½" mortise

⅜" deep, 2⅝" wide dado

2"

2⅝"

5⁄16" x 4" lag screw

1¼" x 5" x ⅜" mortise

1¼" x 5" x ¼" tenon

⅛" dia. hole

1½" x 1½" x 2¾" tenon

Bandsawn kerf, 2" l. ¼" from edge

4½"

2½" r.

3° taper

3 15⁄16"

¾" deep, 1½" wide dado

DETAIL: LEG-TO-RAIL BOLTS

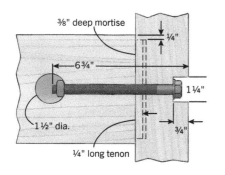

⅜" deep mortise

¼"

6¾"

1¼"

1½" dia.

¾"

¼" long tenon

TOP VIEW

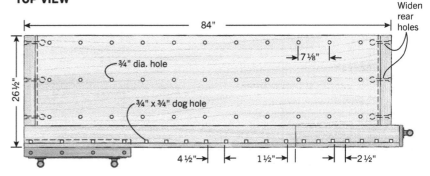

84"

Widen rear holes

26½"

¾" dia. hole

7⅛"

¾" x ¾" dog hole

4½"

1½"

2½"

FRONT VIEW

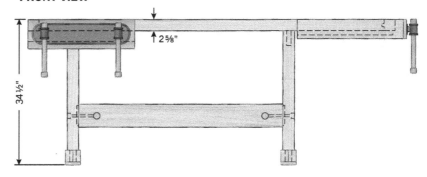

2⅝"

34½"

pieces in stages, over a few days, so they have a chance to stabilize before you mill them to final size.

Mill the legs. Mill pieces for the feet. Note that each foot is glued up from two pieces. Cut dadoes in the feet (they will become mortises for the legs; see illustration at top left). Remove most of the waste using a bandsaw. Next, square the dados on the table saw, using a stop block and spacer. Finally, angle the ends of each dado, so the tenons can flare when wedges are inserted into them. Make two blocks the size of the leg's tenons to register the feet. Glue the feet together. Bandsaw a radius on the front end of each foot.

Cut tenons on the legs. Begin by cutting the tenons' shoulders all the way around each leg, then cut the

cheeks using a tenoning jig. Only one setup is needed, because the legs and tenons are square. Drill ⅛"-diameter holes in the tenons (they prevent the wedges from splitting the legs). Cut slots for the wedges, up to the holes, using the bandsaw. Cut the wedges on the bandsaw, making them extra long. Lay out the open mortises on the top of each leg. Remove most of the waste on the bandsaw and finish the joints using the tenoning jig.

Mill the top stretchers. Assemble the legs and feet, without glue. Clamp a board across the legs to keep the assembly square. Mark the position of the dadoes on the top stretchers directly from the legs. Cut dados on three sides of each joint. Note that the top stretchers will be ⅛" proud of the top of the legs.

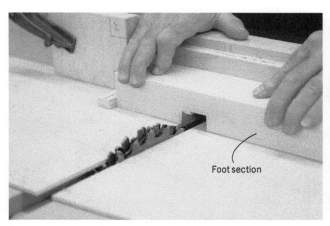

Foot section

Start with the base. The legs are joined to the feet with large through-mortises (see p. 40, Exploded View: Base Joinery). Each foot is composed of two pieces, which will be glued together later on. Begin making the mortises by dadoing each half of the feet.

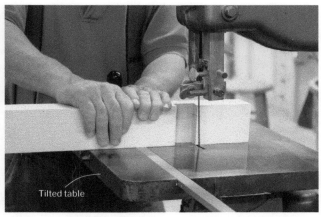

Tilted table

Angle a portion of each dado using the bandsaw. This creates a flared opening for the leg's tenon, which will be secured by wedges.

Mock tenon

Glue together the two pieces of each foot. Insert a mock tenon, covered with clear cellophane packing tape, into the dadoes. Clamp small, taped blocks above and below the feet to align the pieces.

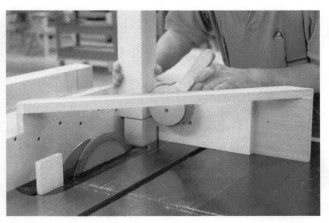

Cut tenons on the legs using a tenoning jig. Using the bandsaw, cut two slots in each tenon to receive the wedges.

Rout mortises for the rails that connect the leg sets. Make a template and cut the mortises using a top-bearing pattern bit. Drill holes in the legs for the bolts that will fasten the rails to the legs (p. 40, Detail: Leg-to-Rail Bolts). Drill holes in the top stretchers for the lag bolts that will be used to fasten the top. Make the rear holes larger than the front holes to allow the top to expand and contract.

Plane, scrape, and sand the legs, feet, and top stretchers. Glue the two leg sets and drive home the wedges. Fasten pads to the feet. (Don't glue them. This allows you to change the bench's height later on.)

Mill the rails. Cut their stub tenons using a dado set. Clamp the rails between the leg sets. Continue the bolt holes by drilling as deep as possible into the rails with a ½" brad-point bit. Disassemble the rails and con-

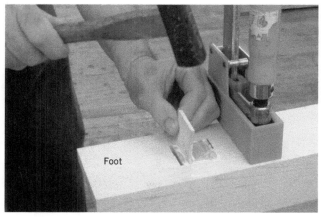

Add stretchers across the top of the legs. Glue the feet to the legs. Drive wedges into the slots to flare the ends of the tenons. These joints will never come loose!

Bolt the base together. The bolts engage square nuts inside the rails.

The benchtop is made from 3"-thick hard maple. Glue the top in two sections. Run each half of the top through the planer to even the glue joints.

Glue the top. Support it on straight wooden bars. Clamp the ends to help align the two halves.

tinue drilling. Insert a bolt into each hole and mark the location of the nut holes in the rails. Drill these holes. Assemble the base.

START THE TOP

Make the main top in two sections of approximately equal width. Each section may be built up from any number of boards you wish. When cutting these 3"-thick boards to width, I use an 18-tooth rip blade to ease the load on my cabinet saw's motor. Joint one face of each board and plane the opposite side. (At this point, it's OK if the planer skips over some areas.) Joint one of the board's edges, rip the board to width, and joint the sawn edge. Glue the boards together. Mill and bring the end caps and the long dog block to final thickness, but leave them 1" extra long. Plane the two glued-up top sections to the same thickness as these pieces. Glue the two top sections using strong bar clamps.

Use a circular saw with a guide to cut the top about ⅛" longer than its final size. Saw from both sides. This top is heavy! To aid in flipping it, clamp a 4' long 2x4 to one end, across the top's width, and use the 2x4 as a lever. Cut the ends of the top to final length using a router and a guide.

Trim the end caps to final length. Using a slot-cutting bit with a 4"-long arbor and a top bearing, cut slots in the end of the top (see p. 43, Detail: End Cap Bolts). Work from both sides of the benchtop to center the slots. Using the table saw, cut tongues on the end caps to fit the slots, again working from both sides. Drill three holes in each end cap for the bolts that secure the caps to the top. Make the front holes tight (⅜"), and drill the two rear holes at a larger diameter (⅝") to allow the top to expand and contract. Clamp the end caps to the bench. Lengthen the holes for the bolts by the same method you used for the rails above. Drill blind holes for the captured nuts.

I use holdfasts and other clamping devices to secure work to my bench. These generally require ¾"-diameter holes, drilled all the way through the top and end caps with a Forstner bit.

INSTALL THE TAIL VISE

I've searched long and hard for sturdy tail vise hardware that's not too difficult to install. The best I've

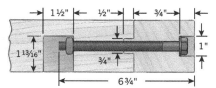

DETAIL: END CAP BOLTS

1 ½" · ½" · ¾"
1 ¹³⁄₁₆" · ¾" · 1"
6 ¾"

Rough-cut the ends of the top. Use a guided circular saw or a standard circular saw following the edge of a board. Cut from both sides.

Make the ends square and smooth. Do this by following up with a router and straight bit. Use a board to guide the cut, which only goes halfway deep. Flip the top and finish the process with a long bottom-bearing bit.

Equip a slot-cutting bit with a long arbor. Make a series of passes to cut a ¾" slot in each end of the benchtop. Then make end caps to fit the slots. The end caps keep the top flat, and are attached with bolts.

Move on to mounting the tail vise. The metal parts are available as a kit. The vise travels on a steel guide plate, which must be precisely located using a shop-made gauge block.

Gauge block

Guide plate

EXPLODED VIEW: TAIL VISE

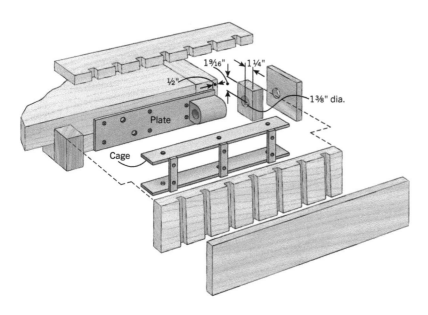

DETAIL: TAIL-VISE PLATE-SPACING JIG

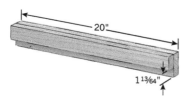

DETAIL: BENCH DOG

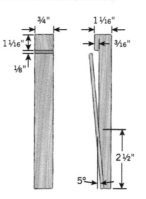

under the end cap, though.) I fasten the plate with machine screws, so it's easier to remove for cleaning and lubrication. Alternatively, you can use a self-centering (Vix-style) bit and #14 flat-head screws. In any case, the plate must be installed precisely parallel to the top of the bench. Make a spacing jig to locate the top of the plate (see far left, Tail-Vise Plate-Spacing Jig). Clamp the jig and plate to the bench, then drill a pilot hole for one screw at one end of the plate. Install the screw, then drill a second hole and install another screw. Remove the gauge block and double-check that the plate is parallel to the top using a combination square. If it's not, remove the second screw and use a different hole in the plate. Drill holes for the remaining screws and install the plate.

Build the tail vise. Mill the top and short dog block to thickness and width, but leave them ¼" extra long. Mill the front jaw and rear blocking. Drill a hole for the vise's screw in the rear blocking. To assist in gluing these parts together, make a 20 ¼"-long spacer. Clamp this block between the front jaw and rear blocking, and then glue up the four pieces you've made. The top and short dog block should overhang ⅛" on both ends. When the glue is dry, trim the top and short dog block flush using a crosscut sled or flush-trim bit.

Next, cut the dog holes in the tail vise. They're angled 2° to the left, while the dog holes in the benchtop will be angled 2° to the right (see p. 45, top right). Cut the dog holes with a dado set using a sled with a 2° wedge screwed to the fence. (To help you make this wedge: A 2° angle rises

found is made in Germany by Dieter Schmid Fine Tools. It consists of a plate that's fastened to the bench and a cage that's fastened to the tail-vise assembly. Note: This hardware is right-handed only.

Begin by fastening the plate to the bench. First, glue a block under the bench, flush with the top's edge, to increase the top's thickness (see above, Tail Vise). (Don't apply glue

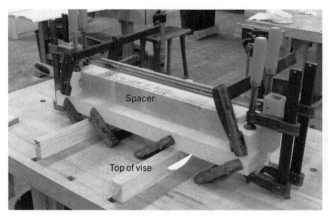

Glue together the end-vise block. Glue and clamp the top, ends, and short dog block of the tail vise. Use a spacer between the ends to ensure that they're the correct distance apart.

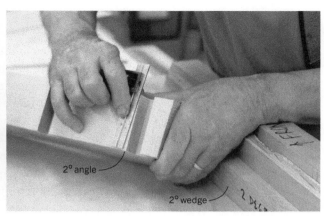

Cut dadoes, angled at 2°, in the tail vise's dog block and top. Use a long wedge to create the angle. These dadoes will become holes for the bench dogs.

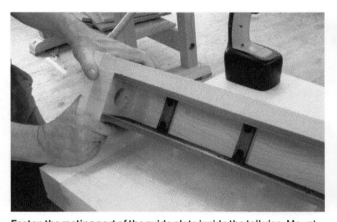

Fasten the mating part of the guide plate inside the tail vise. Mount the assembly on the bench.

Cut dog-hole dadoes in a long block. Lean the opposite way from the dadoes in the tail vise. Glue the block to the benchtop.

about ¾" over 20".) Make the wedge long enough to extend off both ends of your crosscut sled. You'll need this extra length later on for the benchtop's longer dog block. Note that the thin end of the wedge is to the left of the blade, to lean the dadoes the correct way. Clamp the tail-vise cage to the tail-vise assembly, and as before, drill and tap to mount it. Cut, drill, and install the end cap, leaving the overhang on the left, and mount the tail vise. It should be slightly proud of the benchtop, for now.

COMPLETE THE TOP

Next, install the long dog block on the front of the benchtop. To begin, screw the tail vise all the way in. Measure the distance from the front jaw to the left end of the bench—this will be the actual length of the long dog block. Cut the block to length and mark the locations of the dog holes. Be sure to take into account the guide bars and screws of your front vise—you don't want dog holes directly above them. Cut dados in the long block. Reverse the 2° wedge you used above so the

dados lean the right way. Glue the dog hole block to the top.

Mill the front caps for the bench and vise and glue them on. Fasten the top to the base, then plane the caps and the top of the tail vise flush with the top. Make the bench dogs (see p. 44, Bench Dog).

INSTALL THE FRONT VISE

I used a good-quality front vise with twin screws. This vise has a 16 ⅞" opening between its two screws, which are connected by a chain.

Turning one of the vise's handles also turns the other handle, which keeps the front of the vise parallel to the bench as it clamps a workpiece.

Many other types of vises would work well on this bench. Whatever vise you use, its front face should be flush with the front of the bench. If your vise has iron jaws, cut a recess in the back side of the front cap for the vise's rear jaw before gluing the cap to the benchtop.

The vise I used comes with complete mounting instructions, but you'll have to add an additional piece under the benchtop, a rear jaw, to accommodate the vise. Mill this piece, then clamp it to the top and mark where the top's dog holes are located. Cut dados in the back of the rear jaw to align with the dog holes—note which way the dados should lean. Drill holes in the jaw for the vise's screws and glue the jaw to the bench. Plane the jaw flush to the top.

Make the front jaw. Taper it from top to bottom using the planer and a shim. Install the front jaw, screws, and chain. After everything is tight, plane the top of the front jaw flush with the benchtop.

Finish your bench by applying a light coat of thinned shellac. This gives the maple a pleasant amber tone, offers some resistance to stains, and prevents glue from adhering to the top. ■

Complete the benchtop. Glue a face piece on top of the dog block. Glue a similar piece to the front of the tail-vise assembly.

Glue an additional piece below the top. This is in order to mount the face vise. Plane the piece so it's level with the edge of the bench.

Make the front of the face vise. Use a sled and shim to taper its inside surface. This 2° taper ensures that the vise will pinch at the top when it is fully tightened.

Shim

Install the front vise. You can use any kind of vise here—I'm using a twin screw. This design minimizes the amount that the vise will rack from side to side.

CUT LIST & MATERIALS

	NO.	ITEM	DIMENSIONS (INCHES)			MATERIAL*	COMMENTS
			T	W	L		
BASE							
☐	4	Legs	2 5/8"	2 5/8"	31"	12/4	Length includes 2 3/4"-long tenon.
☐	4	Feet	1 3/4"	2 3/4"	25"	8/4	
☐	8	Wedges	3/16"	1 1/2"	2 1/4"	4/4	Taper at 3°.
☐	2	Top stretchers	1 3/4"	3 1/2"	22 1/4"	8/4	
☐	4	Foot pads	3/4"	3 1/2"	3 1/2"	4/4	
☐	2	Rails	1 3/4"	5 1/2"	47 1/4"	8/4	Length includes two 1/4"-long stub tenons.
TOP							
☐	1	Main	2 5/8"	21 1/8"	79"	12/4	Build in two sections, each no wider than planer width.
☐	2	End caps	2 5/8"	3"	21 1/8"	12/4	Plane to same thickness as top.
☐	1	Long dog block	2 5/8"	4 3/8"	62 1/8"	12/4	Plane to same thickness as top.
☐	1	Blocking	1 1/2"	2"	17 1/2"	8/4	
☐	1	Front cap	1"	2 5/8"	62 1/8"	5/4	
TAIL VISE							
☐	1	Top	1"	4 5/16"	23 3/4"	5/4	
☐	1	Short dog block	1 11/16"	3 1/2"	23 3/4"	8/4	
☐	1	Front jaw	2 3/16"	3 1/2"	2"	12/4	
☐	1	Rear blocking	2 5/8"	3 1/2"	1 1/2"	12/4	
☐	1	End cap	3/4"	5 5/16"	4 1/2"	4/4	
☐	1	Front cap	1"	4 1/2"	23 3/4"	5/4	
FRONT VISE							
☐	1	Rear jaw	1 3/4"	4 1/8"	24 3/8"	8/4	
☐	1	Front jaw	2 1/4"	6 7/8"	24 3/8"	12/4	Taper this piece by 2°, across its width, after fitting.
BENCH DOG							
☐	2	Bodies	11/16"	3/4"	6 1/2"	4/4	
☐	2	Springs	1/8"	3/4"	5 11/16"	4/4	
SUPPLIES							
☐	4	Square nuts for leg bolts	1/2"-13				
☐	4	Leg-to-rail bolts	1/2"-13		6 3/4"		
☐	6	End cap bolt nuts	3/8"-16				
☐	6	End cap bolts	3/8"-16		6 3/4"		
☐	1	Large tail vise	2"	3 5/32"	23 1/4"		Such as Dieter Schmid's; 14" screw travel
☐	1	Front vise					Screw centers up to 16 7/8"

* All non-supply parts made from hard maple unless otherwise indicated.

SHAKER WORKBENCH

This stack of drawers and storage under a workbench has Shaker written all over it.

BY GLEN D. HUEY

When I started work at *Popular Woodworking* magazine, my workbench was a couple storage cabinets on wheels and a cut-off slab of solid-core door. The assembled bench design worked, but then again, it wasn't sturdy, solid, or anywhere near going to be the bench that I used for an extended period of time. So, it was decided that I should build a workbench. A Shaker-style workbench jumped to the forefront of the many design choices. I wanted a showy bench. One that when looked at in 100 years, most observers would wonder if it was for use or for show.

To create a Shaker design, I knew that I needed to have doors and a stack of drawers under the benchtop. In keeping with traditional Shaker benches, I planned to paint the under-chassis. But the structural members, as well as the top, had to be tiger maple—over the years, I had accumulated quite a stash of less-than-quality figured wood that would do nicely as a benchtop.

STOUT LEGS AND STURDY MORTISES

Start the construction of the bench with the legs. Instead of searching for 16/4 stock that is milled to 3 ½" square, look for material that can be glued to the required size. Rough-cut eight pieces of 8/4 stock that is 3 ¾" wide x 34" in length. Each leg is made from a pair of these blanks. Because you want a final size of 3 ½", joint only one face of each piece to gain a smooth surface for a good glue joint.

Once the legs are assembled and the glue is dry, mill the pieces to the final dimensions, then begin the layout work to locate the mortises. I oriented the full faces of the legs to the front and rear, keeping each leg's glue line facing the ends of the bench.

The mortises for both ends and the back are identical. Each location receives a 1" x 4 ¼" mortise for a 5"-wide lower rail and a 1" x 2 ¼" mortise for the 3"-wide upper rail. The front legs receive an identical mortise for the 3" lower rail at the base of the leg—the rail beginning at

A furniture joint on the bench. Shaker craftsmen would employ the dovetail joint for the top rail. To maintain strength in the joint, set the socket back from the front edge.

Pin down some strength. The added pins reinforce the joint. Because the size of the dowels match the size of the drill bits, the job couldn't be easier.

2 ½" above the floor. The upper rail is ⅞" thick and 2 ¾" wide. It's a dovetail joint (that's evidence of the furniture maker coming out in me).

There are many ways to cut the mortises. You can make a plywood pattern and use a plunge router and router bit, you can hog out the majority of the waste material with a Forstner bit at the drill press, or you can slave through the work with a mortising chisel and a mallet. I elected to use a dedicated mortise machine. Whichever method you select, cut the mortises to a depth of 1½".

CREATING THE RAILS TO A STRONG JOINT

Once the leg mortises are made, mill the material for your rails. That batch of material should also include the beams that stretch from front to back of the base and add support to the bench (see photo on p. 51). The mortises for those beams are cut into the lower front and back rails. You also need to cut the mortises for the

rear divider that runs between the rails of the back. A quick step back to the mortising stage, then you're ready to cut tenons.

Install a dado stack in the table saw and raise the blade to ⅜". Set the fence to act as a stop for a 1½"-long tenon. Nibble away the waste material on the four surfaces of each rail exposing the tenon. Fine-tune the fit of each tenon into its respective mortise.

The front top rail is joined to the front leg posts with a dovetail joint. Cut the dovetail socket into the top of the legs. Use a handsaw to define the edges of the socket, then use chisels to remove the waste.

With the socket complete, fit the top rail to the legs. Slide the lower-front rail into the front legs, then

FACE FRAME–DRAWER RUNNER JOINERY

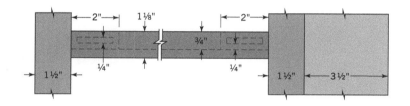

BACK VIEW DETAIL

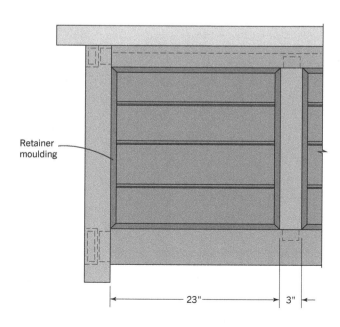

SIDE VIEW

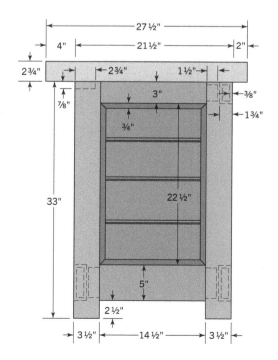

Standing strong and sturdy. All the rails are fit to the legs with mortise-and-tenon joinery. It's possible to simply add a benchtop at this point to have a well-built woodworking bench.

add clamps to secure. Next, scribe the dovetail length onto the front top rail, lay the rail on top of the legs positioning the scribe line at the edge of the legs, and transfer the socket layout onto the rail ends. Saw away the waste material. Carefully fit the dovetail to the sockets to get a tight fit.

ASSEMBLE THE WORKBENCH BASE

Work in stages. Sand the inner portions of the legs and the inside of each rail, then add glue to the mortise-and-tenon joints and assemble the back of the base. Add clamps to secure the assembly. Pin each joint with a ⅜"-diameter dowel. Use two pins in the wide rails and a single pin in the 3" rails.

Next, assemble the bench base's front. I added a #8 x 1½" screw to reinforce each dovetail joint and pinned

the lower rail of the front with a single dowel pin in each joint.

For the ends, glue the rails' tenons into the mortises and pin those joints as well. Don't forget the beams in the bottom of the base. Installing these parts makes the assembly of the base a bit tricky. It's necessary to slide all the joints together at the same time. When complete, the base structure of the workbench is standing strong.

MAKING BEADED PANELS

To achieve a Shaker look on the exterior of the bench, I decided to fill in the open areas between the ends and back with tongue-and-grooved pieces. To add a bit of excitement, I included a bead detail on each piece.

Cut the tongue-and-groove joints at the table saw. First, mill the pieces necessary to fill each opening. Lay out the pieces edge to edge and mark

the edges that get a groove and the mating edges that get a tongue. The starting piece has a groove only, while the ending piece will have a tongue only. All remaining pieces have both a tongue and a groove.

Cut a ¼"-wide groove centered on the edge of the boards. To do this, set the blade height to ⅜" and the area between the fence and the blade at ³⁄₁₆". Make a single pass over the blade, then reverse the board and make a second pass. The result is a ¼"-wide groove that's centered on the edge.

Making the matching tongue is also a job for the table saw. This time, set the blade height to ³⁄₁₆". Making the tongue is a two-step rabbet cut completed on both faces of the piece. Make the first pass with the board lying face down on the table saw surface. Cut both faces of the boards that get a tongue.

Routing a bead detail. The bead detail is placed on the tongue portion of the joint. Cutting the profile on the groove would weaken the joint considerably.

Now, adjust the blade height to ⅜" and position the fence at ⁷⁄₁₆". Cut the boards on edge to finish the tongue. This setup makes the cut so the fall off is not trapped between the blade and the fence, and the result is a ¼" tongue. Slight adjustments might be necessary to obtain an exact fit. The joint should slide together easily without the aid of a mallet or your palms. A joint that's too tight at this stage will present problems later, after paint is applied.

The bead detail is fashioned at the router table with a ¼" beading bit and is cut on the tongue portion of the joint. If the bead were cut onto the groove area, the joint would fail due to material breakage.

Set the height of the beading cutter so the lower edge of the router bit bead profile is aligned with the top edge of the tongue. Rout the detail into each piece that gets a tongue.

Holding the panels in place is accomplished with a combination of backing strips and moldings. The backing strips are ⅝"-thick material attached with screws to the inside edge of the legs and the vertical, back divider, as well as the top and bottom rails. The strips surround the openings and hold the beaded panels in position. The retainer moldings trap the panels and are added after the balance of the base is complete and the panels are painted.

A FLAT-PANEL DIVIDER

The first step to constructing the interior of the bench is to make the vertical flat panel that divides the

FRONT VIEW

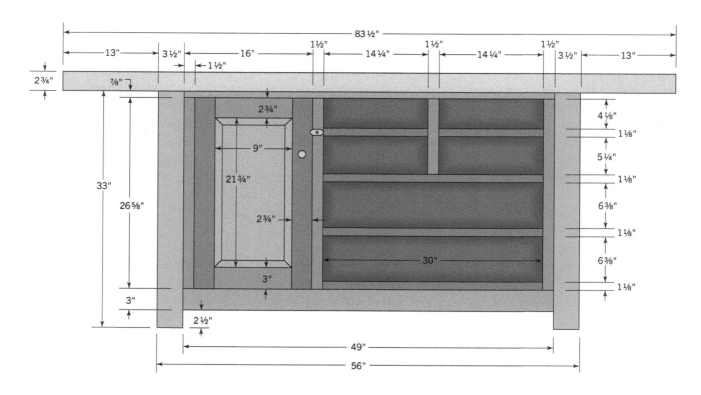

drawer bank from the storage area fronted by a door. The panel is created with rails, stiles, and a floating panel.

Use mortise-and-tenon joints to build this panel. Cut the pieces to size according to the cut list. I use a mortiser to make the ¼"-wide x 2 ¼"-long x 1¼"-deep slots.

Next, cut a ¼"-wide x ⅜"-deep groove on the four pieces of the frame at the table saw (just as the groove on the beaded panels was created). The fence settings are different from the earlier setup due to the thicker stock of the frame.

Cut the matching tenons next. Set the table saw blade to a height of ¼" and set the fence to cut a 1¼"-long tenon. Make the cheek shoulder cuts on each end of the rails, then raise the blade to ⅜" and make an edge shoulder cut on the interior edge of the rails only.

The fence has to be adjusted to make the haunch cut in the outer edge of the rail. Move the fence toward the blade ⅜" and make a second edge-shoulder cut. You can see the haunch appear as the cut is made. The ⅜" offset in the fence matches the depth of the groove. The haunch will fill the plowed-out groove.

To fit a flat panel to the frame, you need to create a series of rabbets along each edge of the panel. The resulting tongue slips into the groove in the frame and is centered on the panel's edges. Set the blade height and fence both at ¼", then run each edge of one side of your panel over the blade. Flip the panel and run the second set of cuts with the same settings.

Next, stand the panel on edge and raise the blade to clear the top edge

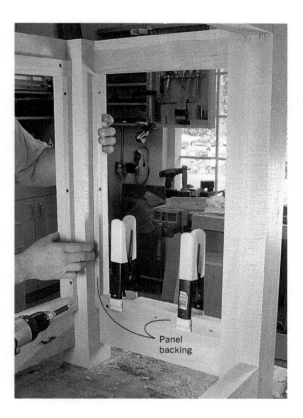

Panel backing

of the previous cut. Adjust the fence to leave ½" between it and the blade. Make the cuts to create the tongue on the panel. Cut all four sides, then reverse the panel to cut the remaining four sides, allowing the tongue to emerge. Add glue to the mortise-and-tenon joints—but not on the floating panel—and assemble the flat-panel divider.

Install the completed divider into the bench base with pocket screws. Two screws are set into the beam of the base and one additional screw is positioned into the top rail of the back. The divider is held to the front of the bench by the face frame, which defines the drawers and storage area.

PUTTING ON YOUR BEST FACE

The face frame for the workbench is built using a series of half-lap joints

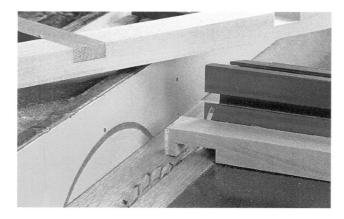

Perhaps the strongest joint. Given the narrow stock used for the face frame, the half-lap joint is stronger by far than a mortise-and-tenon joint would be. This frame will be together a long time.

Precise layout. Matching the center divider to the face frame ensures the fit is correct. It's best to get exact measurements versus using a plan.

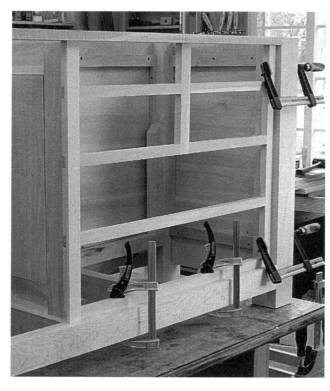

Well-placed clamps. Clamping the face frame to the bench base does not require scads of clamps. Strategic placement and having a square frame guarantee an accurate glue-up.

between the rails and stiles. This joint is strong, and because the face-frame pieces are narrow, this joint offers more strength than a mortise-and-tenon could. The concept is to have the horizontal dividers pass behind the vertical dividers at each half-lap location. Pay attention to detail as you cut these joints.

Begin the half-lap joinery by milling the three vertical dividers, the center divider that splits the top two rows of drawers, and the four drawer dividers. There is no top rail for the face frame—the top front rail of the base acts as the face frame's top rail.

Set the blade height to ⅜". After laying out the location of the drawer dividers according to the plan, use a miter gauge to guide the vertical pieces over the blade to remove the waste material. This requires a number of steps with each half-lap area being nibbled away. Find and cut the half-lap areas into the two drawer dividers for the center divider.

Making the cuts on the drawer divider ends is the easy cut. In fact, you can cut the half-laps at the ends of the drawer dividers and for the lower drawer divider into the three vertical dividers with the same setup.

Slide the fence toward the blade. Leave the appropriate length for the mating part of the joint, but don't change the blade height. Make the first pass over the blade to establish the length, then nibble away the remaining material. Test the joint for both width of cut and fit of the joint. A good half-lap joint finishes the same thickness as the material used in the joint.

To find the location of the half-lap joints in the center divider, it's best to assemble the face frame and position the center divider flush with the top of the face frame assembly. There you can mark the areas that need to be removed for the drawer dividers as well as the overall length of the center divider. Then, it's back to the table saw to complete the joinery. Once the joints are made and fit, add the glue and clamps to assemble the face frame.

The face frame sits back 1" from the front edge of the base rails. Remember to position and glue the vertical divider on the left-hand side of the door. Attach the assembled unit to the base of the workbench with glue and clamps. Also, join the face frame and the flat panel divider with glue and a couple finish nails, which act as clamps while the glue sets. In addition, drive a screw through the bench's top rail into the ends of the vertical face frame pieces.

SUPPORT FOR THE DRAWERS

The face frame divides up the drawer bank, but the drawers run on a web frame that attaches to the backside of the dividers. Each web frame is ¾" thick and the dividers are 1⅛" wide. To work, the frames need to be held flush with the top edge of the dividers. Each frame has a piece at the front called the extension and two runners.

The drawer web frames start with the drawer extension. The extensions run from side-to-side of the drawer opening, bridging the half-lap joints and have ¼"-wide x 1½"-long x ½"-deep mortises cut in each end of the rear edge for the runners' tenons.

The runners begin as 2"-wide stock. Form a ½"-long tenon on one end of each runner while the other end, the end nailed to the rear leg or flat-panel divider, is notched to use a 1½" nail. Once the completed frames

Nails provide the connection. The drawer frames are held in place with nails. Make sure the runners are level by starting at the bottom and measuring each location based off the front divider.

The simple drawer frame. The lower frames for the drawers are quickly completed once the mortises and tenons are made. Assemble the frames and square the runners off the extension.

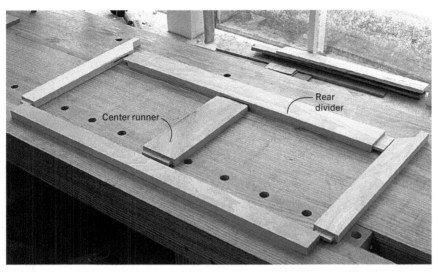

Split drawers add work. The frames for the upper drawers require three additional mortises as well as a rear divider and a center runner—and with mortises come tenons.

Clamps galore. Attaching the rail extensions to the face frame dividers requires many clamps. It's best to stage the process working one frame at a time. Once dry, level and nail the runners at the back.

are in position, measure the location of the rear of the frames then add nails to secure the frames in place.

The lower frames are completed with the attachment of the runners to the extensions. Glue the tenons into the mortises and set the assemblies aside until dry.

However, the upper frames are different. Because the upper two rows of drawers are split, those frames also require a center runner that provides support on either side of the center vertical divider. The drawer extensions for those two rows need to have a third mortise to house the center runner. Position the runner in the center of the opening, not centered across the extension. Because of the center runners, it's necessary to install a rear divider that extends between the runners and fits into mortises placed in the runners. The center runner is attached to the rear divider with a mortise-and-tenon joint as well.

It's important to have plenty of clamps on hand or move through the installation of the frames in steps.

DRAWERS, DOOR, AND TRAYS

The door's frame is built just as the flat-panel divider was earlier. Use mortise-and-tenon joints with a haunch at the corners. The only difference is the door has a raised panel instead of a flat one. Create the raised panel at the table saw or with a raised panel cutter at the router table. Slip the panel into the groove as the door is assembled. Glue only the joints. The door is installed after the finish is applied.

Make the drawers using traditional dovetail joinery. The lipped

Drawer work begins. The table saw allows you to fine-tune the fit of the drawer. Measurements for other drawer parts are based off the inside face of the drawer fronts.

Spacers

Keeping trays level. The pull-out trays need to be level from front to back and from side to side. To ensure that happens, use spacers.

fronts are rabbeted on three sides after the edges are rounded with a ⅜" roundover bit. The balance of the drawer parts are determined from the inside face of those fronts.

The 16"-long drawer sides are the same width as the inside of the fronts from the bottom edge to the start of the rabbet.

The drawer back is ¾" less than the width of the drawer sides—the drawer bottom slides under the back and into grooves in the sides and front—and the length is equal to the inside face of the drawer front from rabbet to rabbet.

Use through-dovetails to join the drawer sides to the backs and half-blind dovetails to join the drawer fronts to the sides. The drawer bottoms are bevel cut at the table saw to slide into a ¼" groove that is plowed into the drawer front and sides prior to assembling the drawer boxes.

The trays that fit into the storage area behind the door operate on full-extension drawer slides. The sides of the trays themselves are 2¾"-wide stock that is joined at the corners with through-dovetails. Remember to correctly size the box. The final width is dependent on the slides selected. The slides used on this project require a ½" of clearance per side, so the tray box is 1" narrower than its opening.

With the tray boxes built and assembled, use brads to attach a ledge around the interior of the box for supporting the removable tray bottoms.

The full-extension slides need to be shimmed from behind so they are flush with the door opening. On the right-hand side, as you face the door, nail ⅝"-thick x 2"-wide material to the flat-panel divider. The area on the left-hand side of the storage area requires 1½"-thick stock to build out for the slides. Screw these to the legs.

The bottom tray is aligned with the top edge of the base rails—just high enough to bypass the rails as the tray is pulled out. The second tray is 12" above the first tray. In order to keep the trays level from front-to-back and side-to-side, use a pair of spacers to position the top tray assembly.

To finish the construction of the base of the bench, add two blocks at the top edge of the ends to provide a method to attach the top. The 1¼"-thick material is fit between the front and rear leg and glued in place.

Counting pieces. The top was laminated from 32 pieces of lumber. Work in stages, please. Trying to laminate all the pieces at once will be a glue-filled mess.

Jointing a flat surface. The stock for the top begins oversized to allow multiple trips to the jointer and planer. Having a level and true benchtop is paramount in bench making.

Picture-frame molding. The panels on the base are held in place by the molding that is installed in picture-frame fashion—the corners are mitered.

A SHOWY BENCHTOP

The top of a workbench is its important feature. This surface receives the most wear and should be solid (and showy) in my view. This bench has a tiger maple top that's 2 ¾" thick. The top is a 32-piece lamination of hardwood that was ripped, milled, and assembled into one heavy slab of lumber.

I ran each piece over the jointer to gain a straight, flat surface, then through the thickness planer to achieve a uniform thickness. From there, they were grouped and glued into three workable sections. Each of the three sections, when removed from the clamps, was once again jointed and planed to be straight, flat, and uniform in thickness. Additionally, the top was surfaced with a wide-belt sander to arrive at the final dimension.

The last step was to assemble the three sections. That left two joints to be worked by hand. Pay particular attention to the joint when gluing the final sections together. Any variations in the joint directly transfer to additional handwork to straighten and level.

The vises selected for your bench are a reflection of your work habits. I like a quick-release vise for both my front and my end vise. Every vise is supplied with installation instructions that should be followed completely.

Drilling round holes for bench dogs—no square-cornered dogs for me—was last on the list prior to beginning the finish. After hearing stories of woodworkers burning up drills or using the man-powered brace and bit and auger, I knew I had to find an easy method to drill my holes. Using the router to drill holes for adjustable shelf pins flashed through my thoughts. Could we apply that same method to the bench? Yes.

Use a ¾" up-cut spiral router bit and the router to plunge-cut those holes. To keep the router positioned as the hole is cut, make a template that traps the base of the router (see photo at right). Clamp the template in place, position the router, then plunge the holes. It's easy. To guarantee accurate hole locations, mark a centerline on the edge of the template and align that mark with the layout lines for your holes.

Drilling in the edge of the benchtop is another mystery to solve. I again used the router, but the surface area was too narrow to plunge cut without concerns. To alleviate any problems, clamp a long guide to the base plate; clamp the guide to the top before plunging the cut. These front holes allow clamping of wide materials in the face vise. The top and base are attached with four 5" hex-head bolts with nuts and washers that are countersunk into the top and extend through the attachment blocks. The bench is now ready for finish.

PAINT AND FINISH

All the panels and materials made in poplar are painted with acrylic latex. That includes the beaded panels, the face frame, the drawer fronts, and the door. Paint two coats on all surfaces, sanding between coats. Once the painting was complete, go back and add the molding to lock in the beaded panels. That molding is installed with mitered corners.

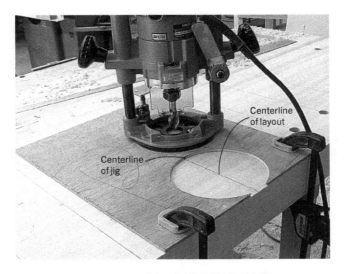

Centerline of layout

Centerline of jig

Jigging up the router. Drilling holes for bench accessories is a task that can kill a drill, but with a plunge router and upcut router bit, the job is short and sweet. Align the centers and rout.

Hold-down holes. A second rigging is needed to drill the holes in the top's front edge. These holes are for accessories that hold wide panels in place.

Popping the grain. Two coats of an oil/varnish mixture is all the protection necessary for the bench. You don't want too much finish on the top. There's no need to have pieces sliding about.

CUT LIST & MATERIALS

	NO.	ITEM	DIMENSIONS (INCHES)			MATERIAL	COMMENTS
			T	W	L		
CARCASE							
☐	4	Legs	3 1/2	3 1/2	33	Tiger maple	
☐	1	Front lower rail	1 3/4	3	52	Tiger maple	1½" TBE*
☐	1	Rear upper rail	1 3/4	3	52	Tiger maple	1½" TBE
☐	1	Rear lower rail	1 3/4	5	52	Tiger maple	1½" TBE
☐	2	End upper rails	1 3/4	3	17 1/2	Tiger maple	1½" TBE
☐	2	End lower rails	1 3/4	5	17 1/2	Tiger maple	1½" TBE
☐	1	Rear divider	1 3/4	3	25 1/2	Tiger maple	1½" TBE
☐	2	Base beams	1 3/4	3	21	Poplar	1½" TBE
☐	1	Front top rail	7/8	2 3/8	51	Tiger maple	1" dovetail both ends
☐	2	Right ext. filler	5/8	2	17 1/4	Poplar	
☐	2	Left ext. filler	1 1/2	2	17 1/4	Poplar	
☐	2	Attachment block	1 1/4	1 1/2	14 1/4	Tiger maple/poplar	
☐	1	Benchtop	2 3/4	27	84	Tiger maple	Laminated
☐	1	Vise block	3 3/8	1 1/2	15 1/2	Tiger maple	
FLAT-PANEL DIVIDER							
☐	2	Stiles	3/4	3	26 1/2	Poplar	
☐	2	Rails	3/4	3	14 1/2	Poplar	1¼" TBE
☐	1	Flat panel	3/4	12 5/8	21 1/8	Poplar	
BEADBOARD PANELS							
☐	2	End panels	5/8	14 7/16	22 3/8	Poplar	Assembled pieces
☐	2	Rear panels	5/8	22 15/16	22 3/8	Poplar	Assembled pieces
☐	1	Retainer molding	3/4	3/4	35'	Tiger maple	
PANEL BACKING							
☐	4	Horizontal ends	5/8	5/8	14 1/2	Poplar	
☐	4	Vertical ends	5/8	5/8	22 1/2	Poplar	
☐	2	Horizontal rears	5/8	5/8	50	Poplar	
☐	4	Vertical rears	5/8	5/8	22 1/2	Poplar	

* TBE = Tenon both ends.

The finish on the top and the tiger maple framing is a mixture I've used for years: one part spar varnish and one part boiled linseed oil (not raw). Keep the wood surface wet for five minutes before wiping away excess. No need to sand between coats; if you skipped wiping an area, sand that spot before applying another coat. Two coats were applied over everything. That's right, everything—including the painted parts of the workbench.

Hang the door using light-duty T-hinges along with a wooden knob and door catch.

I envision many years of building furniture on this bench. I wish I had built a quality workbench years back. Not that it would have improved my work, but maybe my work habits. No more scattering tools in the shop. I now have a workbench that has storage. ■

CUT LIST & MATERIALS, CON'T

	NO.	ITEM	DIMENSIONS (INCHES)			MATERIAL	COMMENTS
			T	W	L		
FACE FRAME & DRAWER FRAMES							
☐	3	Vertical dividers	¾	1 ½	26 ⅝	Poplar	
☐	4	Drawer dividers	¾	1 ⅛	33	Poplar	
☐	1	Center divider	¾	1 ½	11 ¾	Poplar	
☐	4	Rail extensions	¾	1 ¾	31 ½	Poplar	
☐	8	Drawer runners	¾	2	16 ½	Poplar	½" tenon one end
☐	2	Center runners	¾	3 ½	11 ¼	Poplar	½" TBE*
☐	2	Rear dividers	¾	2 ¾	29 ½	Poplar	½" TBE
☐	4	Drawer guides	⅝	¾	15	Poplar	
☐	2	Center guides	⅝	1 ½	15	Poplar	
DOOR							
☐	2	Stiles	¾	2 ¾	26 ½	Poplar	
☐	1	Top rail	¾	2 ¾	11 ½	Poplar	1¼" TBE
☐	1	Bottom rail	¾	3	11 ½	Poplar	1¼" TBE
☐	1	Raised panel	⅝	9 ⅝	21 ¾	Poplar	Fits into ½" grooves in rails
DRAWER FRONTS (OTHER DRAWER PARTS TAKEN FROM THESE SIZES)							
☐	2	Top row	¾	4 ⅛	14 ⅞	Poplar	
☐	2	Second row	¾	5 ½	14 ⅞	Poplar	
☐	1	Third row	¾	6 ⅝	30 ⅝	Poplar	
☐	1	Fourth row	¾	6 ⅝	30 ⅝	Poplar	
TRAYS							
☐	2	Fronts	¾	2 ¾	13 ½	Poplar	
☐	2	Sides	¾	2 ¾	16	Poplar	
☐	2	Bottoms	⅜	12	14 ½	Plywood	
SUPPLIES							
☐	1	Large quick-release vise					
☐	1	Small quick-release vise					
☐	1	Surface clamp					
☐	1	Quart acrylic latex paint					Olde Century Colors, Cupboard Blue
☐	2	Full-extension drawer slide pairs					
☐	2	T hinges for door					

* TBE = Tenon both ends.

KNOCKDOWN ENGLISH WORKBENCH

In two days, you can build this sturdy stowaway bench.

BY CHRISTOPHER SCHWARZ

Many knockdown workbenches suffer from unfortunate compromises. Inexpensive commercial benches that can be knocked down for shipping use skimpy hardware and thin components to reduce shipping weight. The result is that the bench never feels sturdy. Plus, assembly usually takes a good hour.

Custom knockdown benches, on the other hand, are generally sturdier, but they are usually too complex and take considerable time to set up. In other words, most knockdown workbenches are designed to be taken apart only when you move your household. When I designed this bench, I took pains to ensure it was as sturdy as a permanent bench, but could be assembled in about 10 minutes and you would need only one tool to do it.

This design is an English-style workbench sized for an apartment or small shop at 6' long. It's made from construction lumber and uses a basic crochet and holdfasts for workholding. As a result, the lumber bill is minimal. You'll need four 2x12 16' boards and one 1x10 8' board.

I used yellow pine for this bench, but any heavy framing lumber will do, including fir, hemlock, or even spruce. The hardware is also minimal in cost, though you could easily save money by assembling the bench with hardware that is slower to bolt and un-bolt.

ABOUT THE RAW MATERIALS

The core of this workbench is ductile iron mounting plates that are threaded to receive cap screws. This hardware is easy to install and robust. The rest of the hardware is standard off-the-rack stuff from any hardware store. Make sure your lumber has acclimated to your shop before you begin construction. This workbench is made up of flat panels, so having stable wood will make construction easier and will reduce any warping that comes with home-center softwoods.

When I bring a new load of lumber into my shop, I cut it to rough length and sticker it. I have a moisture meter that tells me when the wood is at equilibrium.

If you don't have a moisture meter, just wait a couple of weeks before building the bench. Also, if the end grain of any board feels cooler to the touch than its neighbors, then that board is still wet-ish and giving off moisture. So you might want to give that stick some more time to adjust. This workbench is made up of five major assemblies that bolt together: two end pieces, two aprons, and a top. Each assembly needs some cutting and gluing. Let's start by building the legs.

GLUED-UP LEGS

The joinery for this workbench is mostly glue, screws, and a few notches. All those joints are in the two end assemblies. Each end assembly consists of two legs made by face-gluing two boards together. The act of gluing these two boards together creates a notch for the bench's aprons.

Begin making the end assemblies by gluing the 5 ½"-wide leg parts together for each of the four legs. If you don't own clamps, glue and screw these parts together, then remove the screws after the glue has dried. If you own clamps, I recommend sprinkling a pinch of dry sand on the wet layer of glue between the laminations to prevent the pieces from shifting during the clamping process.

While the glue in the legs is drying, turn your attention to the aprons.

LAMINATED APRONS

Like the legs, the front and rear aprons of the workbench are made by face-gluing two parts together to thicken the piece and create notches for the other assemblies.

Mounted for work. The ductile mounting plates are durable and easy to install.

Short and long. By gluing a short piece and a long piece together, you create a thick leg and the notch for the workbench's apron.

Aprons at work. Here you can see the 2x12 apron glued to the 1x10 interior piece. The legs will then butt against the 1x10.

Each apron consists of a 2x12 glued to a smaller 1x10 piece. The 2x12 is the exterior of the workbench. The 1x10 makes notches for the legs.

The length of the 1x10 is the distance between the left legs of the bench and the right legs. In this 6' workbench, the 1x10 is 45" long. If your bench is longer, make these parts longer.

Glue and affix a 1x10 to its 2x12—and make sure the smaller piece is centered on the length of the larger. I used glue and nails to put these parts together. Any combination of glue, screws, and nails will do.

Once the aprons are assembled, you can then clip the corners of the aprons if you like. The 45° corners are cut 4" from the ends of each apron with a handsaw. The next step is to use the heavy-duty ductile hardware to bolt the legs and aprons together.

Can't miss. By drilling these holes while the pieces are together, you ensure they will mate up again.

HARDWARE INSTALL

Clamp a leg to one of the aprons, making sure the leg is snug against the notch created by the apron's 1x10. Now lay out and drill the counterbore for the washer and the clearance hole for the bolt's shaft. The clearance hole should go all the way through the apron and leg. The counterbore should be deep enough to hold the head of the bolt, the washer, and the lock washer.

Lock the leg and apron together with the hardware. Thread the bolt through a lock washer and then a washer. Push the bolt through the clearance hole. Spin a ductile mounting plate onto the bolt on the other side.

Snug up the mounting plate, then tighten the nut with a socket wrench.

Mounting plates. Here is how the mounting plates look when they are installed. First you tighten the bolts, then you screw the mounting plate down. This way you can't miss.

Once both bolts are snugged up on the leg, you can permanently install the mounting plates with screws. Repeat this process with the other three legs. When you are done, you will have two aprons with their legs attached.

BEEFY BENCHTOP

One of the downsides to many English workbenches is that the top is springy because it is thin or unsupported from below. The traditional solution was to add "bearers" under the benchtop. These cross members ran between the front apron and the rear apron. While they do make the benchtop stouter, I have never liked these tops as much as I like a simple, thick benchtop.

The top surface of the benchtop is made from 2x12s that have been edge-glued to create a flat panel. This benchtop is 22 ½" wide because it is made from two 2x12s. You can make it narrower if you like—an 18"- to 20"-wide bench is stable enough for handwork. Glue up your two planks for your benchtop and cut the top to its finished width and length.

It might be tempting to glue on the second layer of 2x12 to make the benchtop its final thickness. Resist. It is easier to first attach the aprons, legs, and thin top. Then, once you finish building the end assemblies, you will know the exact size of this second top piece and exactly where it will go without measuring.

FEET IN THE AIR

This next step ensures that the end assemblies will be the correct size for the width of your top. Assemble the bench upside down on sawbenches.

Legs and aprons. With the legs and aprons bolted together, you can glue up the parts for the benchtop.

Easy and accurate. I use aluminum angle pieces for winding sticks. I also use them as edge guides for my circular saw. Clamp the aluminum angle to your benchtop and make your cut.

Clamp the aprons to the top and push things around until the legs are square to the underside of the top and the aprons line up with the top all around.

Once you have everything clamped as you like it, you can fit the pieces for the end assemblies that go between the front legs and the back legs. There is a top plate that is the same width as the legs, plus a top stretcher made from a 2x12 that fits between the front apron and the rear apron.

Cut these pieces to fit. Wedge the top plate pieces between the legs and

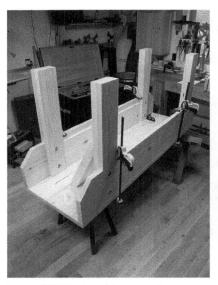

Leg up. With the bench temporarily assembled like this, you can fit the pieces between the legs so they match the space available.

Can't miss II. With the top plate between the legs, you can put each stretcher on with screws (skip the glue because this is a cross-grain construction).

An end, assembled. I know this is an odd construction, but it works. Once you see it, you'll get it. Here you can see the finished end assembly with the lower stretcher ready for trimming and screwing.

3D VIEW

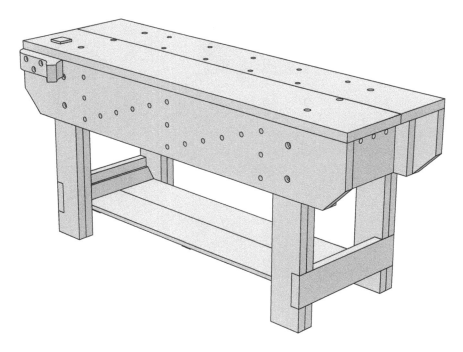

screw the stretchers to the legs. With the top stretchers screwed to the legs, you can take the bench apart, then glue and screw the top plates in place. Don't forget to glue the edge of the top plate to the face of the top stretcher. There is a lot of strength to be found there.

The last bit of work is to attach the lower stretchers to the legs. These stretchers are in a notch in each leg. Cut the notch with a handsaw and clear the waste with a chisel. Then screw and glue the lower stretchers into their notches.

Reassemble the bench's base so you can get the top complete.

THE TOP (AND DETAILS)

With the base assembled, level the top edges of the aprons and the end assemblies so they are coplanar—that's the first step toward a flat benchtop. I dressed these parts with a jointer plane and block plane and checked my work with winding sticks and a straightedge.

Before you put the top on the base, I recommend one little addition at this stage. I attached glue blocks—for the lack of a better word—to the aprons so the end assemblies would be captured. You can see in the photo at right that I used an offcut from a 2x12 and oriented the grain sympathetically with the apron. This five-minute upgrade makes the bench easier to assemble and a bit stouter.

Now, you can flatten the underside of the benchtop by using the bench's base for support.

Put the benchtop on the base and plane the underside of the top flat with a jack plane—don't worry about flattening the top of the benchtop. A couple of F-style clamps on the bench base will keep the top in place during this operation.

Test your benchtop by flipping it over and showing it to the workbench's base. When the two parts meet without any rocking, you are done. Clamp the benchtop in place with the work surface facing up. Install the bolts, washers, and mounting plates through the top and the top plate of the end assemblies. Do this in the same way you attached the legs to the aprons.

Now, flip the assembled bench over. You now can see the precise hole where the second benchtop piece should go. Glue up a panel using 2x12 material and cut it to fit that hole exactly. Glue and screw it to the underside of the benchtop. Then, lift the workbench base off the benchtop

Flat makes flat. If your bench base is twisted, your benchtop will be twisted. It pays to get all the base bits in the same plane.

Bench, flatten thyself. Traverse the underside of the benchtop with a jack plane to get the surface fairly true.

Boring for strength. I put three bolts through each assembly. This keeps things flat. Yellow pine doesn't move much, so I allowed for only a little expansion and contraction by making my clearance holes 1/16" larger than the diameter of my bolts.

and clamp the top pieces together for extra bonding power. When the glue is dry, use a block plane to bevel the mating surfaces so they will slide together easily during assembly.

Overkill. After gluing and screwing the second benchtop piece in place, I also clamped things together while the glue dried.

Apron holes. Here, I'm drawing the diagonal lines for the holdfast holes in the aprons. Many people use wooden pegs in the aprons instead of holdfasts. Both solutions defy gravity just fine.

HOLES AND HOLDING

You just made a table. Now you need to make it a workbench. To do that, you need to add three things: a crochet, a planing stop, and holdfast holes. The holdfast holes restrain your work on the benchtop and front apron. The crochet is for edge planing. The planing stop is for lots of things. Let's make the holdfast holes first.

To lay out the holdfast holes on the aprons, draw two or three rectangles on the aprons between the positions of your bench legs. Two rectangles for a 6' bench; three for an 8' model.

Connect two corners of each rectangle with a diagonal line. Use dividers to equally space six holes from corner to corner on the lines. Then, divide the vertical ends of each rectangle into three using your dividers.

Drill ¾"-diameter through-holes at each of these locations. These holes in the aprons are great for supporting work from below, especially when edge-planing or dovetailing.

Now, lay out the holdfast holes on the benchtop. My preference is to have two rows (you can always add more later). One row is about 3" from the back edge of the benchtop. These should be spaced every 10" to 16", depending on the reach of your holdfast. Make another row of holdfast holes about 6" in front of your back row. These should be spaced similarly, but these holes should be offset from the first row, as shown in the drawings and photos.

Be sure to drill some holdfast holes in the legs—both to store holdfasts and to support large work, such as passageway doors. Hold off on drilling any additional holdfast holes until you really need them.

THE PLANING STOP

The traditional planing stop is a workhorse. I push workpieces against it to saw them, plane them, stick molding on them—you name it. The stop is a piece of dense wood (yellow pine is dense enough) that is friction-fit into a mortise in the benchtop. First, make the mortise; then make the planing stop to fit.

The mortise for the planing stop is right in front of the end assembly and typically 3" or so in from the front edge of the benchtop. This planing stop is 2 ½" x 2 ½" x 12"—a fairly traditional size.

Lay out the mortise on both faces of the benchtop. Bore out most of the waste with a large-diameter bit. Finish the walls with a chisel. It pays to check the walls so they are perfectly square to the benchtop.

Then, plane the planing stop until it is a tight fit in the mortise and requires mallet blows to move up and down. Some planing stops also have a toothy metal bit in the middle that helps restrain your work. You can add that later if you like. It can be a blacksmith-made stop, a piece of scrap metal screwed to the top of the planing stop, or even a few nails that are driven through the stop so their tips poke out.

LE CROCHET

I decided to make a crochet that looks exactly like the one in Roubo's *L'Art du Menuisier*. But to be honest, I don't think the shape matters much. I've used a lot of different shapes over time and they all seem to work fine as long as they are vaguely hook shaped. I made this crochet from scraps. I glued them together, then shaped the

Square hole. This is a great first mortise for a beginning woodworker. Take your time in squaring up the walls.

The hook. You can bolt your crochet on. Some early accounts indicate it was nailed on. You probably could get away with glue alone.

hook on the bandsaw, finishing up with rasps.

I attached the crochet with two lag screws and one cap screw, which was backed by a ductile mounting plate. This allows me to remove the crochet from the apron. As you might notice in the illustration, and in the photo at top right, the crochet slightly interferes with one of the cap screws through the apron. You can avoid this by altering the shape of your crochet or moving the hole for the cap screw.

A SHELF IF YOU LIKE

I always like having a shelf below my bench to store bench planes and other assemblies.

The shelf is a panel resting on cleats that are glued and screwed to the lower stretchers of the end assemblies. You can also screw battens to the underside (or top) of the shelf to keep it flat. The only thing holding the shelf in place is gravity.

AND FINISH

You don't want to make your bench too slippery, so stay away from film

CUT LIST & MATERIALS

	NO.	ITEM	DIMENSIONS (INCHES)			MATERIAL	COMMENTS
			T	W	L		
☐	4	Legs (interior)	1 ½	5 ½	32 ½	Yellow pine	
☐	4	Legs (exterior)	1 ½	5 ½	21 ¼	Yellow pine	
☐	2	Aprons (exterior)	1 ½	11 ¼	72	Yellow pine	
☐	2	Aprons (interior)	¾	10	45	Yellow pine	
☐	1	Benchtop (exterior)	1 ½	22 ½	72	Yellow pine	
☐	1	Benchtop (interior)	1 ½	18	45	Yellow pine	
☐	2	Top stretchers	1 ½	11 ¼	19 ½	Yellow pine	
☐	2	Top plates	1 ½	5 ½	16 ½	Yellow pine	
☐	2	Lower stretchers	1 ½	5 ½	22 ½	Yellow pine	
☐	4	Glue blocks	1 ½	11 ¼	2 ½	Yellow pine	
☐	1	Planing stop	2½	2 ½	12	Yellow pine	
☐	1	Crochet	3	4	12 ⅜	Yellow pine	
☐	1	Shelf	1 ½	16 ½	53	Yellow pine	
☐	2	Cleats	2	2	16 ½	Yellow pine	
☐	3	Battens	1 ½	2	14 ½	Yellow pine	
☐	15	Ductile mounting plates				Iron	For ⅜" x 16 threaded rod
☐	15	Cap screws	⅜-16			High-strength steel	
☐	2	Holdfasts	¾				
☐	20	Flat washers	⅜			Steel	
☐		#10 slot-head screws			1		For mounting plates

SIDE VIEW

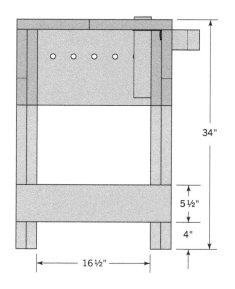

34"

5½"

4"

16½"

finishes (or French polish). I recommend using little or no finish. For most workbenches, I usually just add a coat of boiled linseed oil. You can use an equal blend of oil, varnish, and mineral spirits, or leave the wood bare.

In the end, this really is a remarkably sturdy bench. Most people who use it cannot even tell that it is designed to be knocked down. It is only after they notice the cap screws in the benchtop that they suspect anything. ■

FRONT VIEW

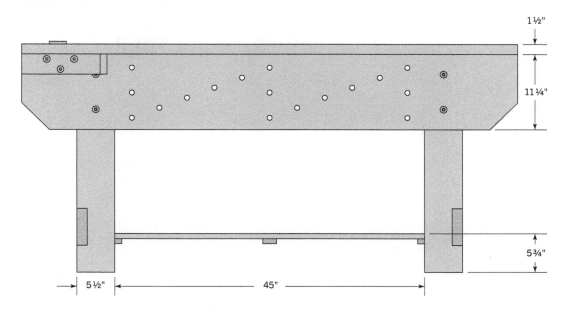

1½"

11¼"

5¾"

5½"

45"

TOP VIEW

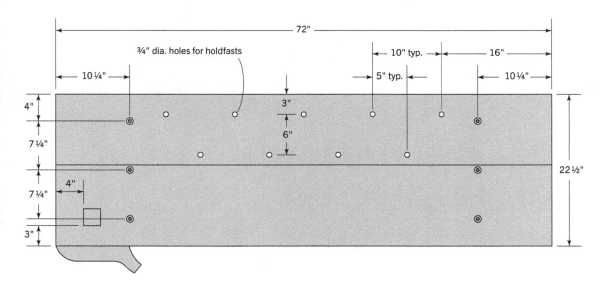

72"

¾" dia. holes for holdfasts

10" typ.

16"

10¼"

5" typ.

10¼"

4"

3"

7¼"

6"

22½"

4"

7¼"

3"

SCANDINAVIAN WORKBENCH

Modern hardware and techniques update this Tage Frid–inspired bench.

BY BILL RAINFORD

Scandinavian- or Continental-style workbenches are the vinyl LP records of the woodworking world. These iconic benches have never left the scene. A few are classics and others are the flavor of the month. Some benches in this style are masterworks and some are poor approximations of an archetypal form. The trick is finding the workbench that hits all the right notes for how you work so you can go on to create your own opus.

WHAT'S OLD IS NEW AGAIN

Much as how Roubo and Nicholson benches have re-surfaced in recent years and have their merits—they were products of their times, the needs of the craftsman, and the avail-ability of wood and hardware—so too has the Scandinavian style of workbench, most popular in the late 19th and 20th centuries. This newer style of bench made use of a changing tool landscape and scarcity of wood,

TOP VIEW

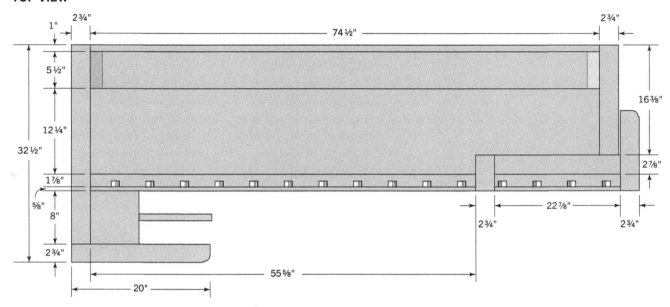

SIDE VIEW

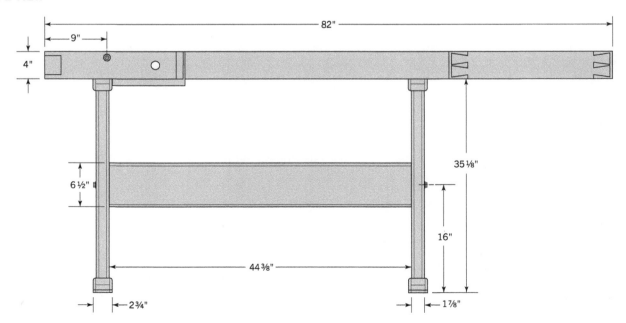

and often required a higher level of skill and/or mechanization to produce. All of those forces are still present in our modern world, where we want to conserve natural resources, mix old and new techniques and tooling, and build something that is both functional and aesthetically pleasing.

When Tage Frid wrote about workbenches in the third volume of his iconic *Tage Frid Teaches Woodworking*, he described a state of time (1948) wherein a good workbench could not be obtained in this country. His solution was to design and build a bench similar to the one he was trained on. Many years later, things are not much better on the retail front, with the majority of mass-produced benches lacking in heft, design, and quality. Thankfully, we've had a

resurgence in traditional woodworking and have a much wider variety of tools, hardware, and literature, making today one of the best times to be a woodworker since World War II.

DESIGN CONSIDERATIONS

My formal training at the North Bennet Street School was on a German workbench in a classroom setting, so when it came time to build my own workbench, I was inspired by Frid's bench—but I also listened to the criticisms. Some folks complained about the relatively short length, which was designed for a modest cabinetmaker in a classroom setting, and the fact that larger folks aggressively planing could potentially move the middle-weight bench around if it wasn't bolted to the floor. Others suggested that the joinery for the

LEFT SIDE VIEW

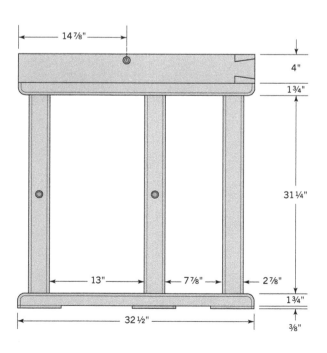

RIGHT SIDE VIEW (END VISE REMOVED)

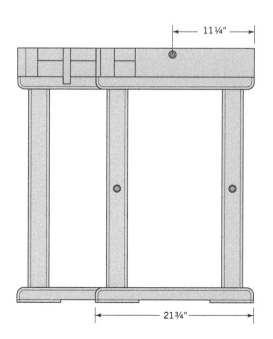

tail vise was too complex, and some noted that the hardware Frid used is no longer available.

To address some of those issues, I made several design modifications and incorporated some new hardware to build a bench that I am very happy with. I have, however, used the same or similar part names, listed in the same order, as Frid did in his book (in case you wish to view them side by side). Here are the highlights of my revised bench:

■ It is almost 2' longer than the original, coming in at about 7' long.

■ It is a few inches wider (making it perfect for my arm span).

■ I incorporated modern hardware—a shoulder and tail vise, square metal bench dogs, bench bolts, slotted washers, and more.

■ The traditional joinery—dovetailed vises and skirt board, wedged tenons, etc.—was cut by hand.

■ I beefed up the stretchers to add additional weight, and decided on larger shoulders to further stiffen the trestle legs to resist racking. (The thicker stretchers also allow me to conceal the bench bolts for a cleaner look.)

SUPPLIES AND RAW MATERIALS

I took my time to select nice, dense, clear, and straight-grained hard maple; it's well-suited for workbench building and relatively plentiful in New England, where I live. Buy your wood well in advance so that you can bring it into your shop, sticker it, and allow it to acclimate to your shop for at least a week. While the wood acclimates, gather all your hardware and vises, and note any changes you need to make to your joinery or design to

fit your hardware. Once the wood is acclimated, plane, rip, and buck the pieces close to their final sizes—but leave them a bit oversized and sticker them again for a couple of days. (If you have a moisture meter, you can monitor the wood as it reaches equilibrium.)

I built the bench in three major assemblies: the benchtop, the trestle legs, and the vises.

BENCHTOP AND SQUARE DOGS

I started with the large slab that makes up the majority of the top surface (it finishes at 1¾" x 12¼" x 74½"). You'll want at least two 8/4 boards for this. If you can't find wide clear stock, you can use three narrower boards to make up the blank. Make sure that the grain is oriented in the same direction for handplaning during the final flattening. Joint the boards, thickness plane them to ⅟₃₂" heavy, then rip a little wider than needed. I used my jointer plane to further true up the edges that will be glued up. At almost 2" thick, the edges provide plenty of glue surface, but I used some biscuits to aid in lining up the pieces and reinforce the joint. Once the glue dries, cut the slab to its final length, making sure to leave sufficient length for the tenons for the end caps.

For the end caps and left vise (the stationary block through which the vise screw rides), I laminated an 8/4 and a 5/4 board to get the required thickness. The 8/4 piece is oriented so it will be in the inside of the joint and receive the groove; the 5/4 piece makes up the exposed face of the piece. Make sure the grain is going in the same direction for ease of planing

Slightly off. With a simple jig, you can rout then repeat for a matching row of dog holes angled at 4°, then square the corners with a chisel. My holes are 1 ³/₁₆" from side to side at the top, and ⅞" front to back—but measure yours off your dogs.

Keep it square.
As you glue on the dog-hole assembly, be sure to attach it square and level to the benchtop.

Slice it clean. Make sure to engage the nicker on your rabbet plane when starting this joint and retract it before the joint reaches its full depth (so as not to cut the fibers in the tenon and weaken the joint).

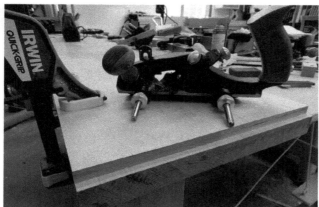

vise lean 4° to the left—the opposite direction to those on the benchtop. Cut these two runs from the same board (with plenty of waste between) and simply flip the jig for the tail-vise portion.

For the 5/4 cap piece that is glued on over the dog holes, choose a clean piece and be careful during your glue-up to avoid getting glue into the slots. I used a pneumatic nailer to shoot a couple of nails into the waste on each of these blanks to ensure things did not move around during clamping. Once the glue is dry, cut the waste off the end of the blank that will be affixed to the benchtop and glue and clamp it to the benchtop. (Here again, I used biscuits to help line everything up.) Make sure to remove any mill marks from the cap.

Once the glue is dry, rip the assembly, at the back edge, to final width (15 ¼" for me) and clean up that edge with a handplane.

BENCHTOP JOINERY

I used a router bit in a router table to cut the grooves on the end caps. But I turned to my skew rabbet plane to cut the rabbets that form the tenons on the ends of the benchtop blank; that was easier than trying to muscle this large assembly onto machinery. The result was a nice, crisp joint with no tear out. Work carefully and test-fit as you go to make sure the end caps fit nicely. At the front of the bench is a spacer block—what Frid called the "left vise filler"—that supports the shoulder vise. To cut the groove for it in the front of the benchtop, after laying out the location with a cutting gauge and knife, I removed the material with a mortising chisel, then

and try to pick clean, clear grain—this will show in the finished bench.

I've worked on benches with square dogs, round dogs, or a mixture of both. I prefer square bench dogs because, in my opinion, they're stronger, taller, have more surface area on the face to engage the wood you're holding, and are less finicky than round ones. (If you prefer round dogs, you can always add a few well-placed ¾" round holes to your bench for them and the holdfasts.) I chose 8/4 stock and used a shopmade template and plunge router to rout the square holes, which are angled 4° to the right off vertical. Note: The slots in the tail cleaned up the stopped dado sides with a wide chisel and the bottom with a router plane.

Next, cut rabbets to form ⅜"-long tenons on both ends and the left side of the filler block. Orient the grain front to back so that when this piece expands and contracts, it does so from left to right, thus expanding into open space rather than into the joint.

The front of the shoulder vise—a 2 ¾"-thick x 4"-wide x 20"-long block, which Frid calls simply the "left vise"—is connected to the left end cap via one massive dovetail (pin on the cap, socket on the vise). I laid that out with a 1:7 ratio and cut it by hand.

After dry-fitting the dovetail, cut a stopped dado in the back of the left vise for the spacer block, then fine-tune the fit (shape the profile on the right end later, after fitting the vise hardware). Now clamp up all the pieces you've cut for the benchtop so far: shoulder vise arm, filler block, main benchtop slab, and both end caps.

Lay out the three bolt holes—one on either end and one through the shoulder vise filler block—that will eventually secure these parts to the benchtop (see the illustrations on p. 74). Take the end caps and shoulder vise arm to the drill press and use a brad-point bit to drill the through-bolt holes, then drill shallow counterbored holes with a Forstner bit to accommodate the bolt heads and washers. Make sure these holes go through the center of the dados on each of these pieces. Re-assemble and clamp the pieces. Using a ⅜" brad-point bit and the hole in the end cap as a guide, drill with a hand drill as far into the top as you can. Remove the end cap and continue the hole using a longer drill bit with some tape to mark the depth; drill the hole a little deeper than the max length you expect the bolt to enter the benchtop. (Note: You'll need a long ⅜" bit or bit extender for these holes.)

When drilling through the shoulder vise filler block, once you get the initial hole started, you might want to remove it from the bench and use a drill press or doweling jig to ensure the hole goes straight through. This

Knife, then cut. Use a cutting gauge and knife to lay out the stopped dado for the left vise filler block (left), then chop it out (right).

Hip to be square. There will be a lot of pressure on this left vise filler block, so you want clean tenons on both ends and the left edge.

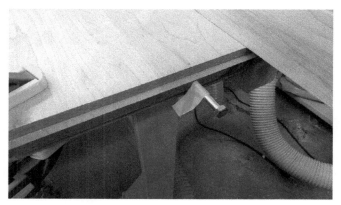

Know your depth. Test the hole depth with a bolt taped off at the max depth you expect it to reach, given the depth it will be into the end cap.

Bolt stretcher. I used anaerobic glue (such as Loctite Threadlocker Red 271) to permanently (I hope!) affix a nut to the end of my threaded rod. The break point for the thread locker was sufficiently high that I could really cinch things down. Use a torque wrench set lower than the break point of the glue and you'll be fine.

Access holes. The size of the holes on the underside of the bench doesn't really matter—they just need to be large enough to accommodate attaching and securing nuts and washers on the ends of the bolts.

On track. A track saw or circular saw with a guide makes quick work of removing the waste where the tail vise goes.

hole needs to pass through the filler block into the dado slot in the bench and into the benchtop. (Make the hole in the filler block a little wider than the bolt to accommodate wood movement; you can correct for a little bit of being off when drilling this hole without affecting the strength of the joint.)

From the underside of the benchtop, lay out the Forstner-bit holes that will accommodate the

square nuts and washer used to secure the ends of the bolts. To make sure they are drilled perpendicular to the bench bottom, I used a portable drill guide with a depth stop. I was not able to find a bolt long enough to go through the shoulder vise support arm, through the support block, and into the benchtop, so I had to make my own from ⅜"-threaded rod by using anaerobic thread-locking glue, such as Loctite Threadlocker Red 271,

Pin layout. When laying out the half-blind dovetails on the rear skirt, make sure the groove for the tool tray falls in a socket, where it will be covered by a tail.

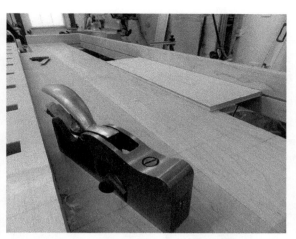

Test-fit. Use a scrap to test the fit of the tool tray bottom to its rabbet. Once you have it dialed in, you use a shoulder plane to fine-tune the joint.

Screw it. Pan-head screws in slots secure the tool tray bottom to the underside of the benchtop.

to secure a nut to one end. (If you go this route, file off any rough edges, because this frozen nut will be visible from the front of the bench.) Re-assemble the benchtop and test out the fit of your bolts.

To cut the top to accommodate the tail vise (and save my back), I used a track saw, then finished up the inside corner of the joint with a handsaw and cleaned it up with a chisel. The rear skirt board is made from 5/4-thick maple. After milling it to size, remove any tool marks with a handplane, then use it as a straight-edge to make sure the end caps terminate at the same point (as they must in order to fit the tool tray).

The ½"-thick plywood tool tray bottom gets rabbeted to fit into a ¼"- wide groove on the inside of this skirt, and is secured on the underside to the bottom of the benchtop with pan-head screws (in slots to accommodate seasonal changes). Lay out and cut this groove (on my bench, it's 1¾" from the top edge), then lay out

the dovetail joint, burying the end of the groove in a socket.

Make the saw cuts by hand, then remove as much waste as you can with a Forstner bit before finishing off the joint with a chisel. Transfer the pin joinery to the skirt board and cut your tails. Strive for tight, clean joints. This skirt board will be held in by tight joinery and some pocket screws—but no glue—in case you ever need to disassemble and repair the bench.

TOOL TRAY
The bottom of the ½"-thick plywood tool tray is 7" wide x 73 ½" long. Cut a ¼"-thick rabbet on the top rear edge to fit the groove in the skirt board. (I recommend using a plywood scrap to test your tooling setup and fine-tune the fit before cutting the rabbet.) On the other edge of the tool tray bottom, saw a series of slots for pan-head screws that will secure it to the bottom of the benchtop and allow for seasonal wood movement.

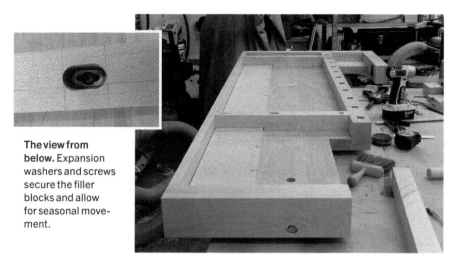

The view from below. Expansion washers and screws secure the filler blocks and allow for seasonal movement.

Tail vise filler. I used the offcut from the vise recess to block in the edge of that recess with 2 ¼"-thick pieces in an L shape—that beefs up the opening to the same thickness as the vise to come. I glued it and pocket screwed it (just in case the glue ever fails).

From some benchtop cutoffs, I made two clean-out ramps (one for either end of the tool tray); screw them in place from underneath, leaving enough of a gap at the ends for seasonal movement of the benchtop.

FILLER BLOCKS

The two "filler blocks" are simply crossmembers that fill the thickness differential between the top of the leg assemblies and the underside of the benchtop. Each 1 ¾" x 2 ¼" x 18 ¼" piece gets a ½" x 6 ¾" notch at the back end to fit under the tool tray bot-

tom. After cutting the filler blocks to shape, mark out their locations, making sure the leg assemblies beneath won't block any of your dog holes. Leave room for the top to expand and contract—this means lateral space between the filler block and the tray bottom and an elongated hole (and expansion washer) securing the block to the rear of the benchtop.

I used heavy-duty 2 ½" pocket-hole screws to secure the top to the filler blocks because they were the only large pan-head screws I could find in the length needed. (You don't need the heavy-duty jig, just the screws and a #3 square driver for this application.) Using a standard pocket-hole jig, I used two ¾" pocket-hole screws to keep the rear skirt firmly attached to the bench.

Using a piece of the benchtop waste from the tail-vise cutout, make a filler block for the tail vise hardware. (Note: This piece does not appear on Frid's bench; it's my modification to accommodate the modern tail-vise hardware.) It's secured with glue and pocket screws.

TRESTLE BASE

Mill the four base pieces to size (a matching pair of each), then cut the ½"-wide x 2 ⅞"-long through-mortises for the leg tenons in the top and bottom pieces before shaping the ends and edges. Drill a hole, 8" from the front, in each top piece for the lag screws that will affix it to the benchtop. Mill the leg pieces to size, cut and fit the tenons on both ends, and mark each to match its mortise. Cut two saw kerfs on the end of each tenon to accept wedges. Now lay out 1"-wide x 5"-long x ½"-deep mor-

Know when to stop. The saw kerfs for the wedges should stop about ¼" above the shoulder.

Beat the clock. Use liquid hide glue to give yourself the long open time needed to get everything together. My 2 ½"-long wedges tapered from ⁵⁄₁₆" to nothing.

Specialty hardware. The 6"-long bolts go into the middle of the stretcher and are secured on the backside of the stretchers with brass barrel nuts.

tises on the inside of four legs for the stretchers. On my legs, the mortises begin 11 ⅜" from the top shoulder; your location will vary if you've adjusted the leg length for a bench of a different height.

Drill ⅜" bolt holes through each of those four legs, centered left to right and top to bottom in the mortises. To remove the mortise waste, I used a Forstner bit to drill out as much waste as possible before finishing up with a chisel and router plane. (Note: The fifth leg supports the shoulder vise and needs no mortise or bolt hole.)

Using a chisel and a planemaker's float, I tapered the top and bottom edges of the mortises a little bit to allow room for the wedged tenons to expand and lock into place.

With the joinery cut, now you can round over the edges.

For the large radii on the ends of the four base pieces, I laid out a pleasing curve using a compass and

pencil, cut off the bulk of the waste at the bandsaw, and cleaned off the mill marks using files and rasps. I eased the bottom edges of the top pieces, and the top edges of the bottom pieces with a ¼"-radius roundover bit in a router.

Before assembling the bases, do a test-fit to make sure you have all the necessary clamps and supplies ready to go. You'll need to work fast in order to assemble this joint and get the wedges driven before the glue sets. Once the glue sets, flush the wedges to the base pieces.

The stretchers on this bench— which are thicker and wider than on Frid's—employ a fully housed tenon (that is, there's a shoulder on all sides) and a set of bench bolts. Mill the stretchers to size, then cut 1"-thick x 5"- wide x ⅜"-long tenons on all four ends. Now lay out and drill 1"-diameter holes on the backs of the stretchers, located 3 ¼" on center from the

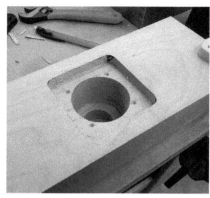

Shoulder vise screw. After drilling a clearance hole (left), use that to locate the plate of the screw hardware, and trace around it. After removing the waste to inset the plate (center), screw the plate in place (right).

Tail vise. Shown here is the vise on its backside. Note the dados in the back of the right vise large filler to accommodate the metal plates of the tail vise hardware, and that they are not all the same. Cut dados to fit your particular vise.

shoulders, and centered top to bottom. These need to be just deep enough to accommodate the bench bolt's large brass barrel nut. Clamp the stretchers in place and use the same technique you used on the end caps to accurately bore ½"-diameter, 6"-deep holes centered in the stretchers.

Screw foot pads to the bottom of the leg assemblies to fine-tune the bench's final height. Note: My pads are ⅜" thick; yours may vary to help keep the base stable on an uneven floor, for example.

Use lag screws (with a washer under the heads) to attach the base assemblies to the filler blocks and let the bench stand on its own for the first time.

SHOULDER VISE HARDWARE

Drill a 1¼"-diameter clearance hole for the Acme-threaded rod of the shoulder vise to pass through the left vise (the dovetailed piece in front). Then, using that hole to orient the fixed nut, trace the outline and screw holes for the nut onto the support arm. Drill a larger hole to accommodate the body of the fixed nut. Then, using a chisel and a router plane, set the fixed nut so that it is flush with the inner surface of the left vise, and secure it with screws.

With the hardware fit, you can dress up the right end of the left vise to suit. I used a skew rabbet plane to create a fillet, then cut an ovolo on the bandsaw and refined it with rasps then sandpaper.

Remount the left vise arm and bolt it in place, then insert the Acme-threaded screw and its handle. Put paraffin wax on the screw threads to make sure it turns easily.

Cut a paddle-shaped 1"-thick x 5"- wide x 16"-long wooden face for the shoulder vise—the left vise jaw (Frid's Part X)—notching it top and bottom at the left end to form a 5 ½"-long tail that fits between the benchtop and top of the trestle legs. (Wax any moving part that rubs wood to wood). Then mount the jaw hardware to the front of it so that it can be removed. The long tail on the face will keep the jaw from falling out, and the flexibility to swap in a customized face for curves or jigs is a nice option to have.

TAIL VISE HARDWARE

For the tail vise jaws, the right dog hole strip, and the right vise cap, lay out and cut large half-blind dovetails (I recommend using the same layout as for the back skirt, for appearance). Drill a hole in the right vise cap for the vise screw. Cut stopped dados in all three of those pieces to accommodate the top filler block and leave room for seasonal movement.

EXPLODED VIEW: SHOULDER VISE

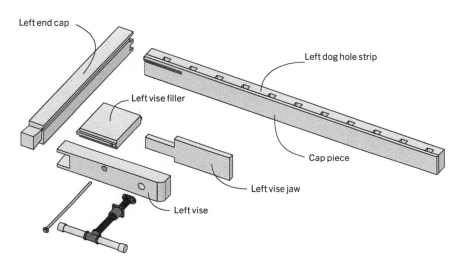

Left end cap

Left dog hole strip

Left vise filler

Cap piece

Left vise jaw

Left vise

EXPLODED VIEW FROM REAR: TAIL VISE

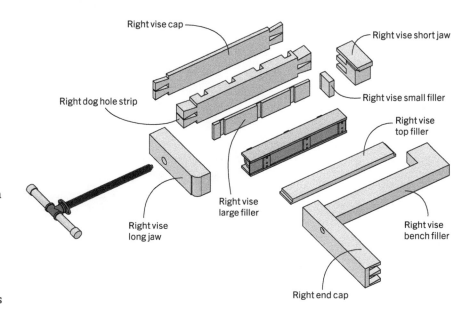

Right vise cap

Right vise short jaw

Right dog hole strip

Right vise small filler

Right vise top filler

Right vise large filler

Right vise bench filler

Right vise long jaw

Right end cap

CUT LIST & MATERIALS

	NO.	ITEM	DIMENSIONS (INCHES)			MATERIAL	COMMENTS
			T	W	L		
CARCASE							
☐	1	Benchtop	1¾	12¾	74½	Hard maple	⅝" TBE*
☐	1	Cap piece	⅝	4	55⅝	Hard maple	
☐	1	Left dog hole strip	1⅞	4	55⅝	Hard maple	
☐	1	Left end cap	¾	2¾	32½	Hard maple	
☐	1	Right end cap	4	2¾	16⅜	Hard maple	
☐	1	Rear skirt board	1	4	77½	Hard maple	
☐	1	Tool tray	½	7	73½	Maple ply	
☐	2	Tool tray ramps	1¾	1¾	5½	Hard maple	
☐	2	Stretchers	1¼	6½	44⅜	Hard maple	⅜" TBE
☐	5	Legs†	1⅞	2⅞	31¼	Hard maple	1¾" TBE
☐	2	Base right	1¾	2¾	21¾	Hard maple	
☐	2	Base left	1¾	2¾	32½	Hard maple	
☐	4	Foot pads	⅜	2¾	6	Hard maple	
☐	2	Filler blocks	1¾	2¼	18¼	Hard maple	½" x 6" notch one end
☐	1	Right dog hole strip	1⅞	4	22⅞	Hard maple	Cut at same time as top strip; reverse jig.
LEFT VISE							
☐	1	Filler block	1¾	7⅜	8¾	Hard maple	⅜" TBE and left side
☐	1	Left vise	2¾	4	20	Hard maple	
☐	1	Vise jaw	1	5	16	Hard maple	

* TBE = Tenon both ends. † Four legs get 1"-wide x 5"-long stretcher mortises centered across width, 11⅜" from top shoulder.

Use pocket screws to keep it flush with the dog block. Add additional fillers as needed to shim the tail vise carriage. Mount the fixed plate of the metal vise to the cutout in the side of the benchtop (the sliding carriage rides on this plate), and mount the sliding carriage to the wooden vise assembly; wax the screw and the areas where the carriage rides along the plate. Also make sure you hog out just enough wood from the left cap to allow you to get the tail vise on and off as needed (see p. 85 photo).

Secure the large Acme screw to the moving portion of the tail vise assembly and mount it to the bench.

Insert the handle and make sure the vise moves easily.

FINAL DETAILS

Flatten the benchtop (I use jack, jointer, and smoothing planes, in that order, with a straightedge to identify high or low spots), making sure to keep the top perpendicular to the front skirt. Break any sharp edges with a block plane and clean up any rough spots with some sandpaper.

An easily renewable oil finish is ideal for a workbench. Linseed oil or tung oil are good choices. I finished my bench with a tung oil varnish on the legs and undersides of the bench

CUT LIST & MATERIALS, CONT'D

	NO.	ITEM	DIMENSIONS (INCHES)			MATERIAL	COMMENTS
			T	W	L		
RIGHT VISE							
☐	1	Cap	5/8	4	22 7/8	Hard maple	
☐	1	Long jaw	2 3/4	4	12	Hard maple	
☐	1	Short jaw	2 3/4	4	5 3/8	Hard maple	
☐	1	Large filler	15/32	3 1/8	17 1/4	Hard maple	
☐	1	Top filler	7/8	2 7/8	18 7/8	Hard maple	
☐	1	Small filler	7/8	3 1/8	2 3/8	Hard maple	
☐	1	Bench filler	2 1/4	5 7/8	21 1/2	Hard maple	L-shape; can make from 2 pieces.
SUPPLIES							
☐	1	Bench screw	1 1/16		15 3/4		
☐	1	Large tail vise	2	3 5/32	23 1/4		
☐	2	Bench dogs				Metal	
☐	2	Vise handles	1-dia.		16 1/8	Wood	
☐	4	Bench bolts	1/2–dia.		6	Steel and brass	
☐		#10 expansion washers		1/2	1		3/16" clearance slot
☐	2	Lag screws	3/8		5		
☐	4	Machine bolts	3/8		6		
☐	1	Threaded rod	3/8		14		
☐		Nuts and washers	3/8				
☐		Pocket screws			1		
☐		Pocket screws			2 1/2		Heavy duty

and skirt, and pure tung oil on the top (I don't want it to be too slick to work comfortably on).

The tried-and-true combination of a shoulder vise, square dogs, and a tail vise is a great setup for traditional woodworking. By building this sort of bench, you are joining the ranks of many classic woodworkers including Tage Frid, Frank Klausz, and countless craftsmen who came before them. As Tage wrote, "Now your bench is completed, and looks so beautiful that you hate to use it. If you take good care of it, working on it but not into it, it should stay beautiful for years." ■

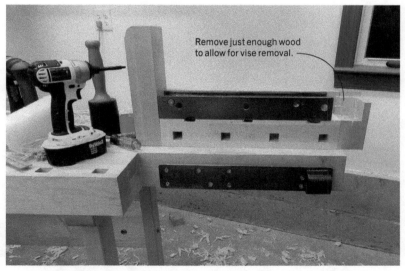

Remove just enough wood to allow for vise removal.

Home stretch. Adjust the screws on the carriage (the piece on the vise assembly) until the tail vise slides smoothly along the fixed plate on the bench cutout.

THE RETURN OF ROUBO

An 18th-century French workbench is quite possibly the most perfect bench design ever put to paper.

BY CHRISTOPHER SCHWARZ

In the 18th century it was common for the workrooms and living areas of a home to share the same space. A workbench, for example, would not be out of place in the front room of the house.

This small historical fact has me concocting a plan, which I haven't yet shared with my family.

My workshop at home is in a walk-out basement. I've done what I can to make it pleasant, but it's isolated from the rest of the house. This is on purpose: My planer and jointer sound like air-raid sirens.

During the brutal stock-preparation phase of a project, my shop is perfect. I can run machinery all day and bother no one. But when I get into the joinery of a project, I long for a shop with beams of natural light, wooden floors, and a close connection to the day-to-day of my household.

In other words, I want to claim some space upstairs as a bench room.

Hold tight: This story isn't just about me. It's about you, too. A furniture-grade workbench is a great idea for apartment dwellers, or people who need to set up a shop in a spare bedroom of their house. It's also a fine idea for people like me who plan

(read: plan to grovel for permission) to do some woodworking in a living area of their home.

Lucky for all of us, one of the best-looking workbench designs is also the simplest to build and most useful, no matter if you have a love affair with your plunge router or your router plane.

THANK YOU, MONSIEUR ROUBO

I've built (or helped build) more than a dozen workbenches based on the 18th-century designs of André J. Roubo, a French cabinetmaker and writer. And after years of working on Roubo's bench, I think it is an ideal bench with almost none of the downsides or limitations I've found on other forms.

Its advantages are numerous. Here are a few.

■ Its simple design makes it easy and quick to build, even for beginners.

■ The thick slab top has no aprons around it, making it easy to clamp anything anywhere on it (this feature cannot be overstated).

■ The front legs and stretchers are flush to the front edge of the benchtop, making it easy to work on

the edges of long boards or assemblies, such as doors.

■ Its massive parts make it heavy and stout. This bench will not rack or move as you work.

But what about its looks? The first Roubo-style workbench I built was out of southern yellow pine. I think it looks great, but an 8'-long pine behemoth might be best suited to the workbench underworld. And it is probably too big for most living areas.

So I decided to go back to the original text for inspiration. You see, the original bench published in plate 11 of *L'Art du Menuisier* shows a bench that has beautiful exposed joinery—through-dovetails and through-tenons in the top. And it has a single piece of wood for its top—something that George Nakashima would love (if it had a bit of bark on it).

In other words, the original Roubo bench has a lot in common with furniture of the Arts & Crafts movement (thanks to its exposed joints), Shaker (with its lack of ornamentation), and even contemporary styles (thanks to the clean lines and use of a single-board top). This bench looks like a lot of furniture that contemporary woodworkers enjoy building and will look at home in the home (if you're lucky) or in the shop.

ABOUT THE RAW MATERIALS

The biggest challenge with this bench is finding the right raw materials, particularly for the top. I was looking for a single slab that was 5" thick, 20" wide, and at least 6' long. That's a tall order. Here are some leads if you'd like to follow suit: Haunt the "building materials" section of online message boards. Old construction beams can be cheap, but you are going to have to scrounge a bit.

You can find a local sawyer (we use a network maintained by Woodmizer). Of course, drying a wet slab that size will take time or some serious work in a kiln. The third option is to find a specialty lumber source, such as Bark House in Spruce Pine,

N.C., which specializes in selling big slabs of kiln-dried lumber and shipping them all over the country.

Almost any species will do for a workbench. Maple or ash would be my first choices, but almost every species is stiff enough and heavy enough to serve as a benchtop when you are dealing with 4"- to 5"-thick boards. I ended up with two slabs of cherry that were donated by housewright Ron Herman of Columbus, Ohio. They had some punky areas and some checks, but I was convinced I could make them into a good-looking top.

For the undercarriage, almost anything will do, as long as it will look nice with the top. I used construction-grade 2x6 white pine for the stretchers and 6x6 mystery wood for the legs. I built the project almost entirely with hand tools (except for

Face your edge. If you are edge jointing two massive slabs into one benchtop, you need to treat the edge of each board more like it is a face. That means checking the surface to ensure it's flat across its width and length. Take your time.

One out of one editors agree. This is a bad idea. Even with my coarsest ripsaw, this slab was too much. After 20 minutes of sweating, I ripped the edge on my bandsaw. The correct tools for this job are a pit saw, a pit and a good strong friend.

Straight up. You can save a ton of work for yourself by checking the slab to ensure it will be flat when it's glued up. A wooden straightedge is ideal for this operation.

a couple long rips). This was for fun. Your definition of fun may vary. All of the techniques here easily translate to a power-tool shop, so don't be put off by the joinery; just fire up your bandsaw.

One other thing to note: You don't need a workbench to build a bench. This entire bench was built on sawhorses without the assistance of any of the benches or vises in our shop.

I began the project by dressing the two rough cherry slabs so I could join their edges to make my benchtop. That's where we'll pick up the story.

TAKE THE TOOL TO THE WORK

The length and the width of your top will determine the rest of the design of the bench. Here are a couple pointers: Make your benchtop as long as feasible, but it doesn't have to be wide (in fact, wide workbenches are a liability in many cases). A 20"-wide bench is plenty big and stable in my experience.

My benchtop required one seam down its middle. To dress the edges, I removed the sawmill marks with a jack plane, then dressed each edge with a jointer plane. Running these edges over the powered jointer would be a two-man job. You can do this by hand by yourself.

Once you get the two edges flat, rest them on top of each other. Look for gaps at the seam and use a straightedge to ensure they create a flat slab. Glue up the top and let it sit overnight no matter what brand of glue you use. You want the glue to reach maximum strength and you want most of the water in the glue to evaporate (if you use a water-based glue, that is).

More than one way to cut a board. Handsaws are designed to be held in a variety of positions, including this one. This position uses different muscles than when you are cutting with the teeth facing the floor. Trying different positions will prevent you from tiring out as quickly.

With the slab joined, dress its outside edges—again handplanes are less effort here than humping this slab over your machines by yourself. After you dress the first edge, make the second one nearly parallel. Then cut the benchtop to length. I used a 7-point crosscut handsaw. It was work, but was fairly quick work.

With the top cut to finished size, dress the benchtop and underside so they are reasonably flat and parallel. Do a good job here because this will be the working surface you'll be using to make the remainder of your bench. Flatness now will prevent struggles later.

Begin flattening the top using traversing strokes across the grain with your jack plane. Follow that up with diagonal strokes with a jointer plane. Or, for the super-lucky, run the slab through your wide-belt sander.

Accuracy on the cheap. I use aluminum angle as winding sticks. These parts are cheap, accurate, and true (unless you abuse them). Paint the ends of one of them black to make the twist easier to see.

No matter how you do it, don't forget to check the top for twist.

Before you get into the legs, it's best to first install your end vise on your top. That way you can use that vise to cut all the joints on the legs. I installed a vintage quick-release vise and added to it a big wooden chop, which will support wide panels on the benchtop.

In addition to the vise, you also should drill the dog holes in the top that line up with the end vise. Place the holes close to the front edge if you use joinery planes with fences (such as rabbet or plow planes). I placed the center of the holes 1¾" from the front edge. Space them closely and evenly—and don't forget to note where the through-dovetails and through-tenons will be. You don't want to put a hole where the joint will go. I spaced my holes on 4" centers. If you can get yours a little closer (say 3"), then you'll be golden.

THE MAGICAL MYSTERY LEGS
I have no idea what species of wood these legs are. I found them in the back of my home center labeled as 6x6 timbers. They were a bit wet and had a few green streaks like poplar. But they were stringy, tough, and difficult to plane. In any case, they were cheap and look pretty good—plus I didn't have to glue up any stock to make the thick legs, which is a nice bonus.

Cut them to rough length (about 1" overlong) with your crosscut hand-saw. The length of your legs determines the height of your workbench. There are many ways to determine your ideal workbench height. My favorite technique is to measure from the floor up to where your pinky joint meets your hand. For me, that measurement is about 34".

If you use hand tools, I would err on the side of a bench that's a little too low rather than too high. Low benches are ideal for handplaning and let you use your leg muscles as much as your arm muscles. Dress the legs with your jack and jointer planes. Prepare to lay out the joinery.

The joints in the legs and top are unusual—each leg has a sliding dove-tail and a tenon. Why did Roubo use a

Small and simple. I used a 7" vintage quick-release vise as my end vise. You can use almost anything, perhaps even a vise you now have.

For looks alone. I added a square ovolo shape to the end of my vise chop. It doesn't have a purpose, except to make the bench look more like a piece of furniture. Cut the shoulders of the ovolo with a backsaw. Use a bow saw to cut the curve and clean it up with rasps and files.

sliding dovetail and not a twin-tenon? I don't know. But based on building the bench, my guess is that the sliding dovetail is easier to cut and prevents that part of the joint from twisting because of the sloped walls.

I spent a couple days (yes, you read that right), poring over Roubo's drawings and the translated French text to lay out the joints so they were balanced and looked like the joints shown in the 18th-century text. I won't bore you with the details (like I bored my spouse), so here's what you need to know:

The sliding dovetail and tenon are each 1¼" thick, with 1" between them. The remainder of the joint is a shoulder on the inside face of the leg. The dovetail is sloped at 1¾" to 1" (about 30°). That's steep, but it looks right compared to Roubo's drawings and other early French benches I've examined.

Lay out the joints. Be sure to make them about ⅛" overlong so you can cut them flush with the benchtop after assembly. Then fetch your biggest tenon saw and a large ripsaw.

Begin by cutting the inside cheek to get warmed up—it's easiest to fix this joint if you go off line. Begin with your tenon saw (mine is a 16" model with about 10 points). First, kerf in the top of the joint in the end grain about ⅛" deep. Cut the cheek diagonally on one side. Turn the leg around and cut diagonally again. Then remove the V-shaped waste between.

When the top of your joint hits the saw's back, switch to a rip-filed handsaw to finish the job. Now do the other cheek of the tenon the same way. Then follow up with the inside cheek of the dovetail.

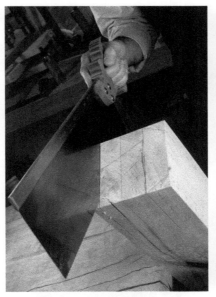

Big, but not big enough. Use a tenon saw to define as much of the cheek as possible by using diagonal cuts. (Or just do it on a well-tuned bandsaw.) When you cannot go any deeper with your tenon saw, it's time to break out the big boy.

I like backless things. Because there is no back on this ripsaw, I can go as deep as I like. Stop sawing when you touch your baseline on both edges.

Connect two. After sawing cheeks across the entire width of the legs, this is easy work. Take your time. Fixing a wandering dovetail slope is no fun.

Cut the dovetail slopes on the outside corners of each leg. Begin with the tenon saw and finish up with the ripsaw. The technique for cutting the dovetail is similar to cutting the tenon. Kerf in the end grain a bit. Then, work diagonally down both edges and remove the stuff between the diagonal cuts.

Heavy metal. A heavy mallet (this one is 2 lbs.) will make the work go faster. Here, I'm almost halfway through the second side and the waste is starting to come loose. Pry it out as soon as it's feasible.

Trace, don't measure. Every leg will be a bit different. Trace the joint layout on the top to get a real idea of the waste you need to remove.

Boring work. Usually I use "boring" as a pun here. This is seriously boring work. A drill press would have been a welcome machine here— though how I would have put this benchtop on the drill press's table is beyond me. I'd probably move the drill press over to the benchtop and swing the table out of the way.

Side-splitting fun. Remove as much of the waste as possible by splitting it off the sides. The wood splits easily along the grain. Knowing the wood's weakness is always a big advantage.

I tried a variety of ways to remove the waste between the dovetail and tenon. The fastest way was to use a mortising chisel. Sawing it out with a bow saw—even a coarse one—was slower. To bash out the waste, treat it like you are removing waste between dovetails. Chisel straight down near your baseline. Then, chisel in diagonally about 1½" away from that first cut to meet your first cut. Pop out this V-shaped piece of waste. Continue until you are halfway through. Flip

the leg over and repeat the process on the second side.

Clean up the bottom of the canyon between the tenon and dovetail. A paring chisel makes short work of flattening the bottom.

Cut the shoulders of the legs. You have three shoulders to cut: Two are up front at the base of the dovetail and the third is at the inside of the leg. I used a crosscut sash saw to make this cut. A smaller carcase saw also would do, but it is slower.

DIFFICULT THROUGH-MORTISES

The through-mortises are some work. Because you are unlikely to have (or want) a 1¼"-wide mortising chisel, you should take a page from our friends the timber framers. Bore out the majority of the waste to excavate the mortise. Then, clean up the walls with a mortising chisel (at the ends) and chisel along the walls.

This job is a good excuse to buy a big brace. While most cabinetmakers will choose a brace with an 8" or 10" sweep, I would recommend a 12" or 14" sweep. You will gain more mechanical advantage. Sadly, my 12" brace went missing, so I gained a workout.

Sharpen the biggest auger you have and mark the flutes so you'll bore about halfway through the top. Clear the holes of waste, then use a mortising chisel to bash out the ends of the mortise (this is the hard and exacting part). Then, use a wide paring chisel to split the remainder of the waste from the walls. This is easy stuff.

Flip the bench over and bore through the other side. Clean up the mortise on the underside and ensure the two cavities meet and have flat walls that are coplanar. (Humps in your mortise walls are common and troubling. Check your work with a combination square.)

Luckily, the dovetail socket is easy work compared to the mortise. Define the walls of the socket using a backsaw (I used a sash saw). Then, take your crosscut handsaw and make several kerfs in the waste. Pop the waste out with a stout chisel and clean the floor of the socket with a router plane and a wide paring chisel.

A CHEAT—BUT NOT WHAT YOU THINK

I made my stretchers using 2x6 material from the home center. After I dressed the stock (it was twisty), it ended up at 1¼" thick. To make life easier I decided to make the tenons on the stretchers by laminating two 2x6s face-to-face. The long one would be the tenons. The short one would be the shoulders between the legs.

A bit of truth here: It's unlikely my legs are perfectly square or their faces are parallel to one another. But if you discard your measuring systems, you'll be OK.

What's critical here is that each stretcher fit perfectly between its legs and end up 3" from the floor. That 3" is the perfect gap for your foot, which you'll find handy (footy, actually) when planing across the grain.

I figured out where the stretchers should intersect the legs and cut two battens to length (21 ⅛" long in this case). I clamped these battens to the legs, rested the stretcher on the battens, and marked my stretchers' finished length directly from the legs. These shoulder lines were not square, but that's no big deal if you cut them with a handsaw.

After I cut these pieces to length with a handsaw I confirmed that they fit between their legs. Then, I laminated them each to a longer section of 2x6. As a result, the stretchers won't have a shoulder at the back (this is called a bare-faced tenon), but that is no big deal in a bench.

The diagonal drill. Think of this like a big angled tenon cheek. Kerf in the top of the joint about ⅛" deep. Then, saw diagonally down until you hit your baseline and the far corner of the benchtop. Go to the other side of the benchtop and work down the other side.

Don't be shy. Make a few kerfs in the waste, then split the bulk of the waste out of the dovetail. Stay about ⅛" away from the baseline to avoid splitting away wood you want to keep.

Router plane reverie. If I could write a love poem to my router plane, I would. It makes tough jobs such as this quite easy. Note you might have to remove the depth adjuster wheel on your tool to reach this depth.

Something for the corners. Your router plane won't reach into the tight inside corners. So—use a paring chisel. Use the flat floor established by your router plane and pare out the junk.

How high? Who cares. I've clamped two battens to my legs and rested the stretcher on them. Now I'm marking the shape of the shoulders directly on the stretcher.

From the inside. Here's what this looks like on my side of the bench. Use a knife for accuracy. Then, cut your stretcher to length with a handsaw.

Almost an instant tenon. Leave the tenons way overlong. They'll be mitered to size after you excavate your mortises.

Mortise without the mess. Here I'm boring out the intersecting mortise, which is deeper than the first mortise. The result is cleaner mortise walls and more surface area for gluing.

MORTISES THAT MEET

When you make mortises that meet inside a leg, there is a tendency to have the inside corner of the joint split when you make the second mortise intersect the first. Does it matter? Probably not much. But I want every bit of wood in there that I can have.

So I use an old English trick for intersecting mortises. Make your first mortise shallow so it will just kiss the second (deeper) mortise. This prevents the inside corner from breaking off.

The mortises in the legs are smaller than those in the top, but the procedure is the same. Bore out most of the waste. Bash out the ends. Pare the long-grain walls. You should be pretty good at this by now.

Miter the ends of your tenons. The tenons don't have to touch—you won't get any points if they do. Then show the mitered tenon to the mortise to mark out the location of the edge cheeks. Saw out the edge cheeks and shoulders. Fit each tenon.

MALLET TIME

Do a dry-fit of all your parts to ensure that not only will the individual joints go together, but that all the joints will go together at the same time. While you could assemble the base and then (if you got lucky) bang the benchtop in place, I think it's better to assemble the whole thing at once.

To hold the joints together, I used drawbored pegs (to pull the shoulders tight to the legs) and a slow-setting, flexible epoxy as insurance. You probably could get away without glue. But, if you can afford the glue, I see no disadvantage to it.

With the bench pieces fit, mark where your ⅜"-diameter pegs will go on the legs. I placed them about 1" from the shoulder of the tenon.

Drawboring is simple: You drill a ⅜" hole through the mortise, assemble the joint, then mark where that hole intersects the tenon. Disassemble the joint, move the centerpoint of the hole about ¹⁄₁₆" or ³⁄₃₂" closer to the shoulder, and drill the ⅜" hole through the tenon.

When you drive the peg in, the offset holes will pull the shoulder tight against the leg. If you have drawbore pins, these metal pins will deform the holes a bit. And they let you test-fit the joint before glue or a peg gets involved in the equation.

A PAUSE BEFORE ASSEMBLY

If you are going to install a leg vise, now is the time to bore the hole for

Again, please don't measure. Hand-cut mortises and tenons are best done by direct comparison. Show the tenon to the mortise (or the mortise to the tenon) and mark what you need.

High and dry. When the bench parts finally go together, the result is remarkably stout, even without glue.

Mortise holes first. The ⅜" holes pass entirely through the legs and mortises. Be sure to stagger the holes if you are going to peg all four stretchers; otherwise, the pegs will collide.

Mark the tenon. Use the same ⅜" bit for boring the holes to mark their center points on the tenons. Then, disassemble the joint.

Move the bore. Shift the centerpoint toward the shoulder of the tenon. When building benches in softwood this can be about ³⁄₃₂" without (much) danger.

the vise screw and the mortise for the parallel guide. This is no different than any of the other mortises in the project, so details here would be redundant.

There are a couple design considerations: Make the center of your vise screw about 10" or so from the top of your workbench. This will allow you to clamp 12"-wide stock in the leg vise with ease. Also, you have a lot of flexibility as to where you put the parallel guide. I've put it at the floor (for maximum leverage) and above the stretchers (for minimum stooping). There isn't a noticeable difference in leverage when you move the parallel guide up, so I'd put it above the stretcher. It's easier to reach that way.

Another design detail: Keep your mortise for your parallel guide fairly close in size to the guide without rubbing or binding (yes, this takes fiddling). A close fit reduces the amount of racking that the vise's chop will do left and right. Trust me on this.

BIG FINISH
When I assemble something, I don't take chances. If I can clamp it, I will.

And if I can glue it, I will (unless it will cause wood movement problems). So, I used some slow-setting epoxy, which has a practical open time of several hours. I applied glue to all the joints, knocked everything together, then applied the clamps to get things as tight as possible.

I drove in the ⅜" white oak pegs. A couple details of these pegs: The best way to get them is to make them yourself. Rive them and drive them through a dowel plate. Whittle one end so it looks like a pencil. Apply some paraffin to lubricate the pin and knock it home. The paraffin is another timber-frame trick that works well. Since I started using it, I've had far fewer exploding pegs.

After driving your pegs, wedge the through-tenons through the top. I used wedges that have a 4° point. Once the glue sets up, remove the clamps and saw the wedges and tops of the tenons flush to the benchtop.

True up the top again, just like you did at the beginning of the project. Then you can turn your attention to the face vise.

Clamps and drawbores. This might seem like wearing both a belt and suspenders, but it will reduce the number of splintered pegs.

And wedges, too. Roubo specifies that you should wedge the tenons that protrude through the top. I declare this joint bomb-proof.

LEG VISES FOR THE WIN

Leg vises are awesome. You can customize them for your work. You can build them in a day. They have tremendous holding power. And they don't have the parallel bars that iron vises use, so you have more clamping real estate.

Why have they almost vanished? Beats me. Most people who try them, love them.

The vises have three parts: The handmade chop, which grips the work; the vise screw (usually a purchased item), which moves the chop in and out; and the handmade parallel guide, which pivots the chop against your work.

The parallel guide is the thing that trips up most people who are new to leg vises. The parallel guide is attached to the chop and moves in and out of a mortise in the leg. A pin pierces the parallel guide in one of its many holes. When the pin contacts the leg, the chop pivots toward the benchtop and clamps your work.

Leg vise setup. Here you can see the parallel guide right before I'm about to install it in the chop. And you can see the hole I chopped out for the vise screw. It's simpler than it sounds.

One setup for the shelf. My shelf boards are 1" thick. I set my plow plane to make a ½"-wide x ⅜"-deep rabbet. A minute of work on each edge made the perfect joint.

Once you make your chop, you'll need to make an orifice for the vise screw and a mortise for the parallel guide. The parallel guide is wedged into the chop and is pierced by two rows of ⅜" holes that are on 1" centers. The two rows are offset by ½".

I know, all this sounds complicated. It's not. I built my first leg vise years ago without ever having used one. Within 30 seconds I had mastered it. You will, too.

A PLACE FOR PLANES

You need a shelf. Let me repeat that: You really need a shelf. You'll put your bench planes there, plus parts and tools that you need later on in a project. Build the shelf; you'll be glad you did.

The shelf takes just a couple hours to build by hand (less if you slay electrons in your shop). Begin by fastening a 1x1 cleat to the bottom inside edge of the four stretchers. I used glue and cut nails. Then you'll nail

shiplapped shelf boards to these cleats to create the nesting place for your bench planes.

To make the shiplapped boards, use a plow plane to make the rabbets on the long edges. This is easy work in pine. I went the extra step and beaded one long edge to dress up the boards. The two boards on the end will need to be notched at the corners to fit around the legs. You know what to do.

Nail the shelf boards in place with about 1/16" gap between each. A single

TOP VIEW

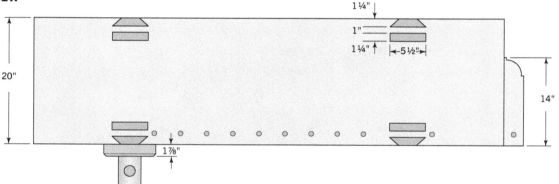

FRONT VIEW

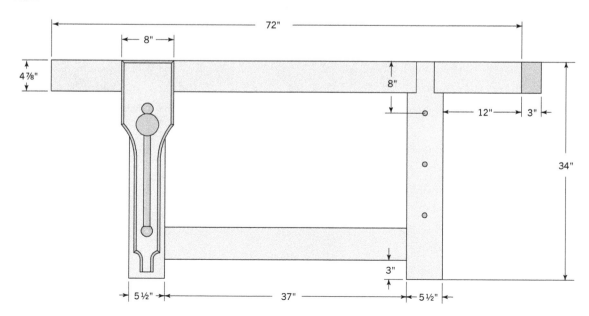

nail in the middle of the width of each board is best. This will prevent your good work from splitting.

A SIMPLER FINISH

Finishes on workbenches should be functional, not flashy. You need a finish that is easy to renew, resists glue and stains, and doesn't make the bench too slick. Slick benches stink.

The answer is so easy. Mix equal parts boiled linseed oil (to resist glue), varnish (to resist spills), and paint thinner (to make it easy to apply). Shake up the amber liquid and rag it on. Three coats is all you need. When it is dry, you can get to work.

When I invest my time in something, I want it to be both beautiful and functional (thank you Gustav Stickley for that line).

So whether this bench goes in the dankest dungeon or in your living room, I think you should do your best to ensure that all your work is ready for the front room of your house. ■

DETAIL: LOWER LEG

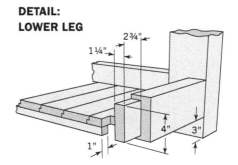

SIDE VIEW

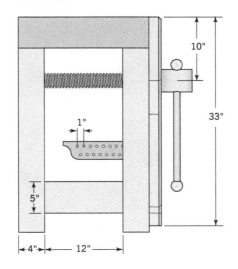

DETAIL: LEG VISE

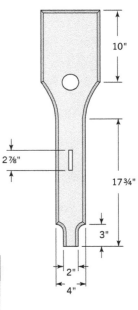

CUT LIST & MATERIALS

	NO.	ITEM	DIMENSIONS (INCHES)			MATERIAL	COMMENTS
			T	W	L		
☐	1	Top	4 7/8	20	72	Maple, ash, or cherry	
☐	4	Legs	5 1/2	4	34	White pine	
☐	2	Long stretchers	2 1/2	5	45 1/2	White pine	4 1/4" TBE*
☐	2	Short stretchers	2 1/2	5	17 1/2	White pine	2 3/4" TBE*
☐	1	End vise				White pine	
☐	1	End vise chop	3	4 7/8	14	White pine	
☐	2	Long cleats	1	1	37	White pine	
☐	2	Short cleats	1	1	12	White pine	
☐		Shelf pieces	1	15	43	White pine	
☐	1	Leg vise chop	1 7/8	8	33	White pine	
☐	1	Leg vise parallel guide	1/2	2 7/8	15	White pine	
☐		Pegs	3/8–dia.			White oak	
* TBE = Tenon both ends.							

POWER TOOL WORKBENCH

This unique project is a traditional workbench, an outfeed table, and an assembly bench—all in one.

BY CHRISTOPHER SCHWARZ

I n a world dominated by power tools, it's a wonder that commercial workbenches are still designed mostly for handwork. These European-style monsters are set up more for planing, mortising, and dovetailing, rather than routing, biscuiting, and nailing.

What's worse, most traditional benches are too big (most are 6' long) for the handwork necessary in a modern garage shop; and they are too small (usually 24" deep) to assemble sizable projects on. Plus, there's the high cost.

One of our contributing editors, Glen Huey, found a solution to this problem when he set up his professional cabinet shop years ago. Glen does some handwork, but for the most part, his motto is: "If you can't do it on a table saw, it isn't worth doing."

So Glen set up his bench as part of his table saw. It attached to the outfeed side of his saw and served as:

- a smaller, traditional workbench for handwork;
- a spacious and solid outfeed table;

- an enormous assembly bench (when you take into account the table saw and its platform);
- and a cavernous place for tool storage in the drawers and on the large shelf underneath the top.

I've watched Glen build dozens of projects with this rig—everything from corner cabinets to a drop-lid secretary—and it has never disappointed him.

I took Glen's great idea and tuned it up a bit with an enormous tail vise, bench dogs, and an extra shelf. I built this bench using southern yellow pine for the top, legs, and stretchers, and I used birch plywood for the tool box. (If you can't locate yellow pine, substitute fir.) The total cost of the wood, hardware, and vise was less than half the price of an entry-level commercial workbench (at that time). If that's still too rich, see the story "Build a Bench—Keep the Change" (p. 110) for more ideas to cut the cost.

As shown, this bench is designed for a Delta Unisaw equipped with the short 30" fence rails. By lengthening the bench's legs up to 3", you can accommodate any table saw on the

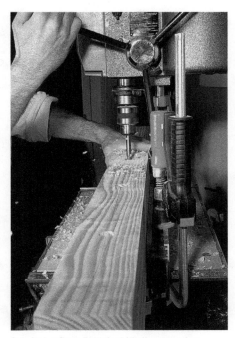

Dog holes first. Drill the ¾"-diameter dog holes into the front edge of your bench before you put the top together. This will save you from making a jig later or having dog holes that wander if you cut them freehand.

Benchtop. I built the top in four-board sections and then glued those sections together. Don't skimp on the glue or clamps, unless you want a big old gap in your bench's top.

market today with the same shopping list and basic bench design.

When completed and attached to your saw, this bench will give you a huge area for project assembly—more than 19 square feet. I call it the "assembly acre."

If you have a contractor-style saw, this bench can be adapted easily to accommodate the motor hanging out the back. If you build the bench without the toolbox, the legs will clear the motor with no changes to the design for most contractor-style saws. I checked half a dozen right-tilt contractor saws to make sure this is true. If your saw is the exception, all you have to do is shift the top left before attaching it to the base. If you want some storage beneath, I suggest making one bank of drawers for the left side only and leave the right side open for the motor.

No matter which bench you build, it will change the way you work.

You can assemble large cabinets on the saw and bench instead of on the floor or driveway. You will have a dedicated outfeed table for your saw instead of a tipsy roller stand. And you will have a bench for handwork that has all the bells and whistles. With a set of bench dogs, an excellent tail vise will handle every common clamping and holding chore. So let's get started.

START AT THE TOP

If you don't have a workbench, build the top first, throw that on sawhorses, and construct the rest of the bench there. The first task at hand is to cut down your six 12'-long 2x8s into manageable lengths. Here's how I did it.

With five of the 2x8s, crosscut them at 54" and 108". Then rip all the pieces down the middle. This will give you the 20 boards you need to make the top. You then can glue up eight of the shorter fall-off pieces face-to-face to make the bench's four legs, and use the remaining two fall-off pieces for the end rails. With the sixth 2x8, you can get the front and back rails, a couple more end rails, and have some scrap left over for cutting test joints.

If you have a planer and jointer, dress all the wood so it's true and then cut it to final size on your table saw. If you don't have these machines, use your saw to rip off the rounded edges. Now borrow some extra clamps from your neighbor and make sure you have a lot of glue on hand. It's time to assemble the top.

Here's some hard-won advice for you on these tops: Assemble the top a few boards at a time. Yes, it takes longer, but the result will be a top

CUT LIST & MATERIALS

	NO.	ITEM	DIMENSIONS (INCHES)			MATERIAL	COMMENTS
			T	W	L		
BENCH							
☐	1	Top*	3	26	52	SYP†	
☐	4	Legs	2 ½	2 ½	31	SYP	
☐	4	End rails	1 ⅜	3	22	SYP	1 ¼" TBE‡
☐	2	Front and back rails	1 ⅜	7	40	SYP	¾" TBE
☐		Joint pegs	⅜ dia.			Dowel	
☐	4	Bench bolts	½-13		6		
☐	1	Twin-screw vise					Up to 16 ⅞" center
☐	2	Vise jaws	1 ¾	7 ⅛	26	Maple	
TOOLBOX CASE							
☐	2	Sides	¾	23 ⅝	16	Plywood	¾" x ½" rabbet for back
☐	2	Top and bottom	¾	23 ⅝	37	Plywood	¾" x ½" rabbet for back
☐	1	Divider	¾	14 ½	22 ⅞	Plywood	
☐	1	Back	¾	15 ½	38	Plywood	
☐		Iron-on edge tape	¾			Birch	
TOOLBOX DRAWERS							
☐	2	Upper false fronts	¾	6 ½	18 ⅛	Plywood	
☐	4	Upper sides	½	5 ½	21 ½	Plywood	½" x ¼" rabbet on ends
☐	2	Upper fronts	½	5 ½	16 ⅝	Plywood	
☐	2	Upper backs	½	4 ¾	16 ⅝	Plywood	
☐	2	Upper bottoms	½	16 ⅝	21 ¼	Plywood	In ½" x ¼" groove.
☐	2	Lower false fronts	¾	8	18 ⅛	Plywood	
☐	4	Lower sides	½	7	21 ½	Plywood	½" x ¼" rabbet on ends
☐	2	Lower fronts	½	7	16 ⅝	Plywood	
☐	2	Lower backs	½	6 ¼	16 ⅝	Plywood	
☐	2	Lower bottoms	½	16 ⅝	21 ¼	Plywood	In ½" x ¼" groove.
☐	4	Full-extension drawer slide pairs		20			

* The top is made from 20 individual boards. With most of the 2x material, I managed to get 1 ⅜" of usable thickness; some boards were a bit corkscrewed and ended up thinner. † SYP = Southern yellow pine. ‡ TBE = Tenon both ends.

that has no gaps between the boards and is more likely to be flat in the end. Assemble your top four boards at a time, using plenty of glue and clamps (I needed almost three 8-ounce bottles for the job). Here's one more tip: If you are going to flatten the top using a hand plane (as opposed to a belt sander), arrange all the boards for the top with the grain running in the same direction. This will reduce any tear out when planing.

After the glue has dried on each section, it's a good idea to dress each assembled section of your top with your jointer and planer. This will make assembling the top easier and the end result a lot flatter. If you don't

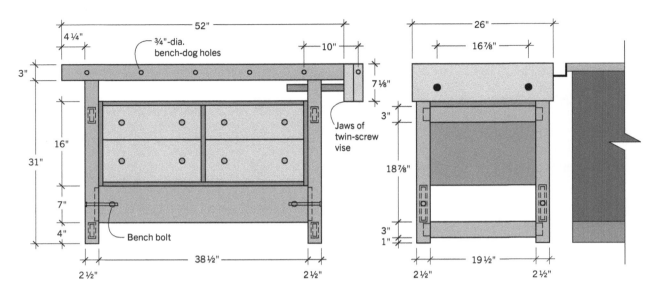

FRONT VIEW

52"

4 ¼"

¾"-dia.
bench-dog holes

10"

3"

16"

31"

7"

4"

Bench bolt

38 ½"

2 ½"

2 ½"

7 ⅛"

Jaws of
twin-screw
vise

SIDE VIEW

26"

16 ⅞"

3"

18 ⅞"

3"
1"

19 ½"

2 ½"

2 ½"

have these machines, be careful during your glue-ups and flatten the entire top at the end. Before you glue all the sections together, pick out the section that will be the front and drill the ¾"-diameter dog holes for the front edge. It's much easier now than when the top is assembled.

After drilling those dog holes, glue the five sections together, clamp, and wait for things to dry.

A MORTISE-AND-TENON BASE

The base of this bench is built entirely using mortise-and-tenon joints. The two ends are glued and assembled using an old-school process called "drawboring," which I'll show you how to do. The ends are attached to the front and back rails using an unglued mortise-and-tenon joint and bench bolts, which essentially are heavy-duty knockdown pieces of

Easy mortise. The easiest way to make clean mortises using your drill press is to first drill a series of overlapping holes (left). Then go back and clean up the waste between these holes several times until the bit can slide left to right in the mortise without stopping (right). Then you only have to square up the ends with a chisel.

hardware similar to bed bolts. These bolts are better than any glued joint and can be tightened throughout the life span of the bench.

The first step is to make a practice mortise in a piece of scrap that you can use to size all your tenons. I made my mortises on a drill press using a ¾"-diameter Forstner bit and a fence. You can make amazingly clean mortises this way. See the photos above for details. After you've made your test mortise, head to the table saw to make the tenons.

I make my tenons using a dado stack in my table saw. The fence determines the length of the tenon; the height of the dado blades determines the measurement of the tenons' shoulders. Set the height of the dado stack to ⁵⁄₁₆", cut a tenon on scrap as shown in the photos below, and see if it fits your test mortise. If the fit is firm and smooth, cut all the tenons on the front, back, and end rails.

Now use your tenons to lay out the locations of your mortises on your legs. Use the diagrams as a guide. Cut your mortises using your drill press. Now get ready to assemble the ends.

TOP VIEW

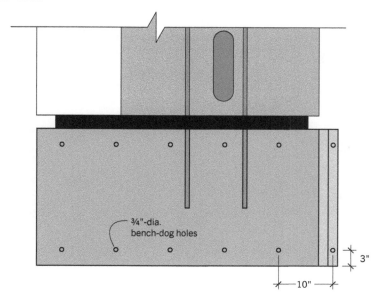

¾"-dia. bench-dog holes

3"

10"

TOP VIEW (TOP REMOVED)

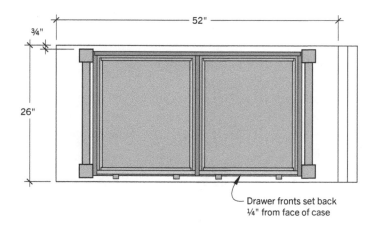

¾"

52"

26"

Drawer fronts set back ¼" from face of case

Dado stack. I like this method because it requires only one saw setup to make all the cuts on a tenon. First, define the tenon's face cheeks and shoulders (left). Define the edge cheeks and shoulders (center). Finally, check your work using the test mortise you cut earlier (right).

SIDE VIEW: DRAWBORING FOR BENCH BOLTS

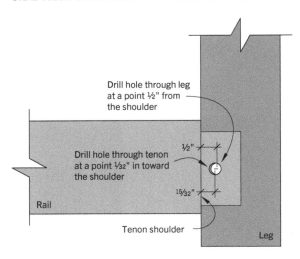

Drill hole through leg at a point ½" from the shoulder

Drill hole through tenon at a point 1/32" in toward the shoulder

½"

15/32"

Rail

Tenon shoulder

Leg

FRONT VIEW: DRAWBORING FOR BENCH BOLTS

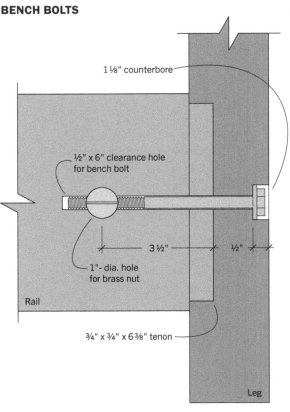

1⅛" counterbore

½" x 6" clearance hole for bench bolt

3½"

½"

1"- dia. hole for brass nut

Rail

¾" x ¾" x 6⅜" tenon

Leg

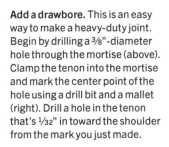

Add a drawbore. This is an easy way to make a heavy-duty joint. Begin by drilling a ⅜"-diameter hole through the mortise (above). Clamp the tenon into the mortise and mark the center point of the hole using a drill bit and a mallet (right). Drill a hole in the tenon that's 1/32" in toward the shoulder from the mark you just made.

DRAWBORING EXPLAINED

Before glues were as reliable as they are today, 18th-century craftsmen would drawbore a mortise-and-tenon joint to get a more mechanical fit. It's not at all difficult to do and reduces the chance of having a gap in your joint, too.

The key to a drawbored joint is a wooden peg or dowel that pulls the tenon into the mortise. Begin by drilling a ⅜"-diameter hole for the peg through the mortise only, as shown in the photo at top left. The hole should be located ½" from the edge of the leg and go just a little deeper than the wall of the mortise.

Assemble the joint without glue and clamp it up. Take a ⅜"-diameter brad-point bit and place it in the hole you just drilled. Use a mallet to lightly strike the bit to mark the center of the hole on the tenon's cheek. Remove the tenon and make a mark for a hole through the tenon that's in the same location as the mark you just made but ¹⁄₃₂" closer to the tenon's shoulder as shown in the left illustration on page 106.

Drill a ⅜"-diameter hole through the tenon at that second mark. When you are ready to assemble the ends you will glue and clamp up the end rails between the legs, put some glue in the holes, and then pound in some ⅜"-diameter dowels. The offset holes will pull the joint together instantly. Hold off on this final assembly step until after the bench bolts are installed.

BENCH BOLTS ARE FOREVER

The set of bench bolts for this project seem pricey, but they are worth it. They are easier to install than traditional bed bolts. And they are much easier to install than using off-the-rack hex bolts, nuts, and washers.

Begin installing the bench bolts by drilling a 1⅛"-diameter counterbore in the legs that's ½" deep. Then drill a ½"-diameter hole in the center of that counterbore that goes all the way through the leg and into the mortise. Dry-assemble the ends and the front and back rails and clamp everything together. Use a ½" brad-point drill bit to mark the center of your hole on the end of each tenon.

Disassemble the bench and clamp the front rail to the top or in a vise. Use a doweling jig and a ½" drill bit

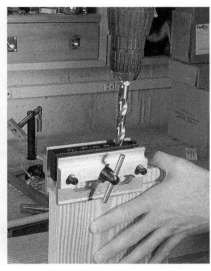

Make a mark. Once you've drilled the counterbore and the through-hole for the bench bolt, mark its location on the end of the tenon using a brad-point bit.

Bench bolt hole. Drill a hole for the bench bolt using a doweling jig and a ½"-diameter drill bit. It's a deep hole, so you might need an extra-long bit to do the job.

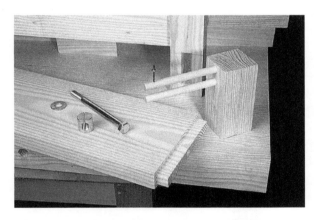

Scrap wood jig. To accurately position the hole for the brass nut, build a simple jig like the one shown here using ½" dowel, a scrap of wood, and a nail. The nail is located where you want the center of the brass nut to go (top). Insert the dowel into the hole in the rail and tap the nail (bottom). Now drill a 1"-diameter hole there and your joint will go together with ease.

Divider placement. I nailed the divider in place in the toolbox so I could check and double-check its position before fixing it in place.

Slide spacers. Use spacers to position your drawer slides for installation. They take an extra few minutes to make, but they act like a third hand when securing the slides to the case.

to continue cutting the hole for the bench bolt. You'll need to drill about 3 ½" into the rail. Repeat this process on the other tenons.

Now you need to drill a 1"-diameter hole that intersects the ½" hole you just drilled in the rail. This 1"-diameter hole holds a special round nut that pulls everything together. To accurately locate where this 1" hole should be, I made a simple jig shown in the bottom photos on page 107 that I picked up from the instruction book for the vise. It works like a charm. Sometimes drill bits can wander— even when guided by a doweling jig— and this jig ensures your success.

Plane or sand all your legs and rails and assemble the bench's base. Attach the top to the base. You can glue dowels in the top of the legs and drill holes in the underside of the top, or you can use metal desktop fasteners with 2 ½"-long screws. Either way, be sure to leave some way for the top to expand and contract.

THE MODERN TOOLBOX
After all that traditional joinery, I was ready to fire up the biscuit joiner. You can build this toolbox using one sheet of ¾" plywood and one sheet of ½" plywood.

Cut your parts to size and start construction by cutting a ¾" x ½" rabbet on the back edge of the sides, top, and bottom to hold the back. The best way to do this is on your table saw. Cut biscuit slots to join these four parts, then glue and clamp up the case. Once the glue is dry, cut the case divider to its finished size, position it inside the case, and nail it in place. Screw the back into its rabbet and apply iron-on birch edge tape to cover the plywood edges. Screw the toolbox to the front rail and legs of the bench's base.

Build the drawers using ½"-thick plywood. Most drawers have ¼"-thick bottom panels, but because these drawers have to stand up to extra abuse, I chose to use ½" plywood instead.

With the drawer boxes built, it's time to hang them in the case. Installing drawer slides is easy if you know a couple tricks. Most professionals simply will scribe a line on the inside of the case and screw the slide there. You'd do it this way too if you installed slides every day. For the rest of us, it's easier to make spacers using scrap plywood that hold the slide in position as you screw it to the case. Install the slides for the top drawer first. Put your spacer in place and put the slide on top. Screw it in place using the holes that allow you to adjust the slide forward and back.

Now install the slides on the drawer sides using the holes that allow you to adjust the slide up and down. Put the drawer in the case and check your work. Adjust the slides and, when satisfied, add a few more screws to lock that position in place. Hang the remainder of the drawers.

FALSE DRAWER FRONTS

Installing false fronts also can be tricky with inset drawers such as these. The best two tools for the job are some shims that you can buy at any home center and the drawer-front adjusters that install on the back side of the false fronts.

Begin by ironing on edge tape to the plywood edges (if desired) and installing the screws for the drawers' knobs. Get set to install the false

Here you can see a drawer-front adjuster installed in the back side of a false front. The machine screw can wiggle a bit in the plastic housing, which allows you to move the drawer front slightly for a perfect fit. Here's a tip: You can plane the white plastic easily if the adjuster isn't flush with the false front.

Position screws. Drill two pilot holes in the drawer boxes and install screws in them so the points stick out about 1/16". Position your drawer front where you want it using shims.

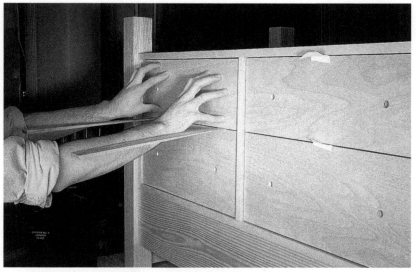

Mark the drawer fronts. Once your drawer front is in position, press it against the screw tips. This will mark the wood for the location of your drawer-front adjusters.

fronts on the lower drawers. Remove the drawer boxes from the top of the case and clamp the false fronts to the lower drawer boxes. Using the shims, adjust the false fronts until you have a 1/16" gap on the sides and bottom. You might have to trim the false fronts a bit using a plane or sandpaper for a good fit. Once satisfied, nail the false fronts in place, then secure them with a few screws.

BUILD A BENCH—KEEP THE CHANGE

Buying a decent workbench will set you back a pretty penny. We built the deluxe bench in this article that is just as heavy, useful, and bulletproof for a fraction of that price; and here's three ways to build it for even less.

- Less-Expensive Vise: Make the bench with a simpler face vise (10 1/2" x 21" overall with a 1 1/8"-diameter screw, and 13" clamping capacity) instead of a twin-screw vise; make your own bench dogs.
- Nice Vise, No Toolbox: Make the bench without the toolbox and make your own bench dogs.
- Total-Economy Model: Make the bench with the less-expensive vise, no toolbox, and use hex bolts instead of the bench bolts
- (8) 3/8"-16 x 6" hex bolts
- (8) 3/8"-16 hex nuts
- (16) 5/16" washers

EXPLODED VIEW: BOX DRAWER

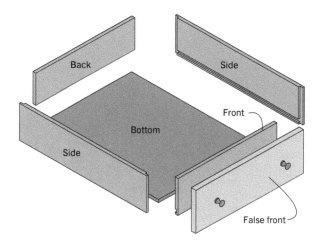

Now put the top drawer boxes back into the case. Drill a couple pilot holes into the front of the drawer box and put screws into the holes so the points poke out about 1/16". Take a top drawer false front and carefully put it into position; add shims to get it close. Press the false front against the drawer box until the screw points bite into your false front. Remove the false fronts.

Drill 25mm holes in the back of the false front for the drawer-front adjusters and pound them in place (see photos, p. 109). Replace the screws in your drawer box with the screws for the drawer-front adjusters and attach the false front. You'll be able to shift the false fronts around a bit until you get a consistent gap all around. When you're happy, add a couple more screws to lock the false front in position.

DETAILS: DOGS AND THE VISE

The spacing of the 3/4"-diameter dog holes on the top of the bench are determined by the type of vise you purchase. The vise I used works best with dog holes every 10" as shown in the diagrams. Chamfer the openings of the holes. You can purchase bench dogs, or make your own dogs by gluing a 3/4" dowel into a small block of 3/4"-thick wood.

Installing the tail vise is a project unto itself and requires a long afternoon and some precision drilling. There should be instructions supplied with the vise, so there's no need to go into detail here. If you mount a twin-screw vise as shown, it's remarkably versatile. This type of vise excels at clamping boards so you can work on their ends, such as when dovetailing.

With the dogs, you can clamp large panels to your bench for sanding. And with the dog holes drilled on the front edge of the bench and vise as shown, you can secure long boards (up to 61" long) to work on their edges.

If your work is both long and wide (for instance, a large cabinet door), you can pull out one of the drawers in the toolbox for additional support while you work on its edge. The drawer slides are rated to hold up to 100 pounds, so you should be able to tackle all but the heaviest panels.

One of your last acts on this bench is to flatten the top. I removed the high spots with a No. 7 jointer plane, cutting diagonally across the top in both directions. Then I cleaned up my work with a random-orbit sander. Check your progress occasionally using a straightedge or winding sticks. A belt sander will take the place of a jointer plane, if you prefer.

Once you load up the toolbox with tools, it's not going anywhere, so there's little need to attach it to the back of your saw. If you do find yourself pushing the bench around, you could add a shelf between the front and back rails of the bench base (below the toolbox) and load that up with more tools or sand bags. Or you can cobble up a way to attach the bench to your saw's table board and sheet-metal frame.

Once you get your bench where you like it, you'll want to rout out a couple channels in the bench's top to accommodate your miter gauge's bar. For my saw, these slots measured ⅜" deep, 1⅛" wide, and 10" long. Measure the bar of your miter gauge with the longest bar and add a little extra for good measure. ∎

CROSS SECTION: DRAWER

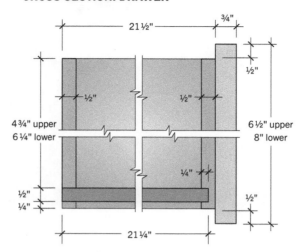

TOP VIEW: DRAWER

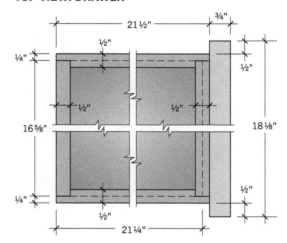

I-BEAM WORK ISLAND

This bit of plywood engineering can serve as a stout base for almost any kind of workbench or shop table.

BY NICK ENGLER

I seem to be setting up a lot of workshops lately. So far, our little band of pioneer aviators have set up two shops in Dayton, Ohio, where we are manufacturing the parts of Wright airplanes and assembling them, and a third shop in Kitty Hawk, N.C., which serves as a repair station to take care of the inevitable wing-dings these primitive aircraft suffer when you fly them. And because the heart of any good shop is its workbench, I seem to be building a lot of benches as well.

With time and materials at a premium, I've developed a simple and economical design for a bench that we use in these shops. It's strong, true, offers loads of storage, and with the addition of a few casters, can serve as a movable work island. We find this last feature especially important, because we must constantly reconfigure the shops as the Wright airplanes grow during construction.

A SANDWICH OF I-BEAMS
The base of the bench is made entirely of ¾" plywood. The plywood parts form three "I-beams," each beam consisting of two caps and a center beam. The shelves and dividers in the bench make up two small I-beams—the shelves become the caps and the dividers are the beams. These are sandwiched together inside a large I-beam that consists of the two workbench ends (the caps) and a center divider (the beam). The resulting structure is very strong.

It's also very true; another important characteristic of a good bench. The benchtop should be flat if you are going to use it for precision work. I cut up the plywood sheets so the factory edge—the outside edge of the plywood as it comes from the factory—is the top of the center divider and the top of the two ends. As a rule, factory edges are pretty straight even if they appear a bit rough. When I attach the benchtop to the base and draw it down tight, the factory edges brace the top perfectly flat.

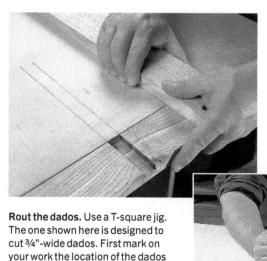

Rout the dados. Use a T-square jig. The one shown here is designed to cut ¾"-wide dados. First mark on your work the location of the dados (above). Line up the dado that's plowed in the T-square jig with your lines. Clamp the jig in place, set the depth of the cut on your router, and make the dado (right).

MAKING THE SANDWICH
The bench can be made almost any size—it's only limited by the size of the sheet materials you use. The dimensions shown in the plans are just suggestions—make the bench whatever size you need. Most craftsmen, I know, will immediately want to make the top a bit higher—34" is somewhat low for a work surface for most people. But it works for me because I'm a short guy.

Once you've decided on the overall dimensions of the bench, cut the plywood parts and rout a few dados to help you assemble and align the parts. Cut the bench ends with three intersecting dados in each—one vertical dado to hold the center divider and two horizontal dadoes to hold the shelves. Make each of these dadoes ¾" wide and ¼" deep. Also make ¼"-deep dados in the shelves to hold the shelving dividers. Then rout horizontal dadoes in the center divider, ¾" wide and ⅛" deep. You must make these dados on both sides of the center divider—that's why they're only ⅛" deep.

PHOTOS BY AL PARRISH

Assemble the base parts with glue and screws; use pocket screws to attach the shelves to the center divider. To make sure that the top edges of the ends and center divider remain true to one another while the glue dries, stretch two strings diagonally from the outside corner of one cap to the outside corner of the other.

The two strings should cross the base, forming a large X. The strings should just kiss each other where they cross over the center divider, and they should rest lightly on the edge of the divider. If the strings aren't laying properly, level the parts of the work-

bench's base with small wedges and shims before the glue dries.

TOPPING THE SANDWICH

You can put a variety of tops on this base—I've used both butcher-block tops made from rock maple and less-expensive tops laminated from particleboard and hardboard. Any hard material about 1½" to 2" thick will do. To attach the top, screw wooden cleats to the center divider and the ends, flush with the top edges. Position the top over the base and drive screws through the cleats and up into your top piece. When the

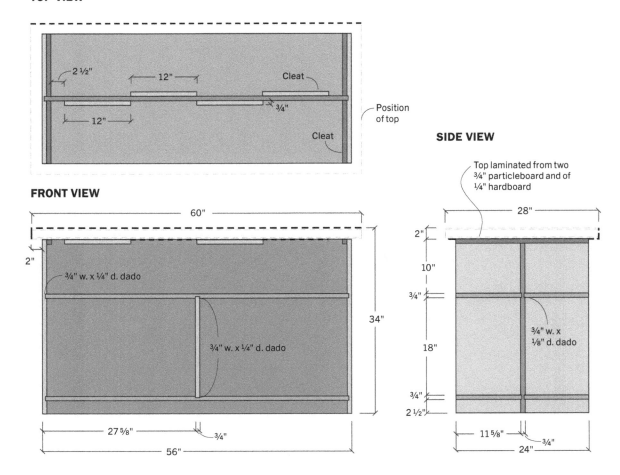

TOP VIEW

2½" 12" Cleat ¾" 12" Position of top Cleat

FRONT VIEW

60" 2" ¾" w. x ¼" d. dado ¾" w. x ¼" d. dado 34" 27 ⅝" ¾" 56"

SIDE VIEW

Top laminated from two ¾" particleboard and of ¼" hardboard

28" 2" 10" ¾" ¾" w. x ⅛" d. dado 18" ¾" 2½" 11 ⅝" ¾" 24" surface gets dirty, simply remove the screws from the cleats, flip over the surface, and reattach.

You can customize this work island to serve your own needs with vises, work lamps, and other workbench accessories. The first thing I usually add are swivel casters to make the bench easy to move. If you want more shelves, drill ¼"-diameter holes in the ends and shelving dividers for shelving support pins, then rest the shelves on the pins. To add drawers, mount guide rails to the ends and divider, then build wooden boxes to slide on the rails. ■

CUT LIST & MATERIALS

	NO.	ITEM	DIMENSIONS (INCHES)			MATERIAL
			T	W	L	
☐	2	Base ends	¾	24	32	Plywood
☐	1	Base center divider	¾	32	56	Plywood
☐	1	Top	2	28	60	Wood*
☐	4	Top cleats	¾	1	12	Plywood
☐	4	Shelves	¾	11⅝	56	Plywood
☐	2†	Dividers	¾	11⅝	18	Plywood

* Laminated particleboard or hardboard, or butcher-block top. † More can be added.

EXPLODED VIEW

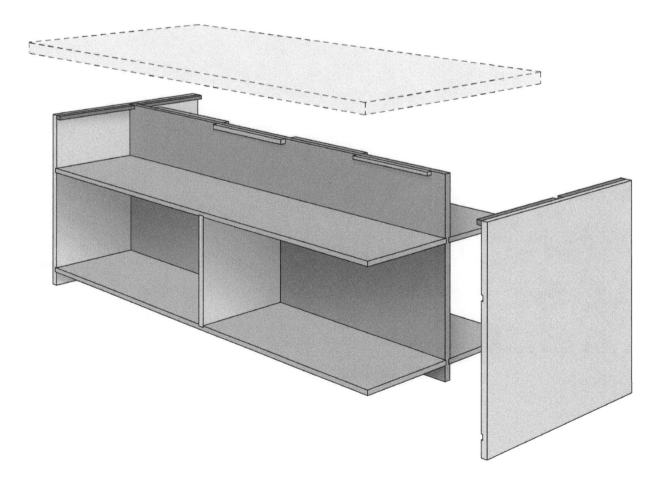

MOBILE ASSEMBLY TABLE

Storage and utility that is just the right size.

BY WILLIE SANDRY

It's often said that a shop layout is never truly complete. While that may be true, I have discovered a valuable asset in my shop that can move and adapt to changing layouts. I've been testing a mobile shop cart over the last several years to make sure it holds up to the rigors of woodworking. The key is middle dividers that act like the webbing of an I-beam. With this tested construction technique, the entire cart forms a rigid base to support the top. The work surface is a double-layer of thick MDF, forming a flat top that can handle daily use and abuse in a shop environment. Special features include pass-through doors, slide-proof adjustable shelves, and a built-in clamp rack for even greater utility.

CONSTRUCT THE BASE

Cut plywood parts to size, and complete the basic joinery shown in the detail rendering (p. 121). Start with the bottom panel, which has a dado to receive the middle divider. Cut 6" wide x ¾" notches at the top corners of the middle divider. These notches will eventually receive long cleat strips, which function to lock the dividers square. Install the end panels, which are rabbeted to fit over the bottom panel.

As you install the first end panel, you'll capture the clamp rack wall in vertical grooves. Add a bead of glue to the bottom of the clamp rack wall component and reinforce this butt joint with screws from the bottom. Now add the other end panel, and glue and nail it in place with 18-gauge brad nails. Finally, add the cleat strips to lock everything in place. The cleats are screwed into the middle divider

The main case. The end panels are rabbeted to fit over the bottom panel, and the middle divider sits in a shallow dado. The clamp rack wall is also housed in grooves on both sides. Glue the main case together, and add the cleat strips to lock it square.

Pocket holes. Secure these long strips flush to the end panels with three pocket hole screws. Add glue to reinforce this butt joint.

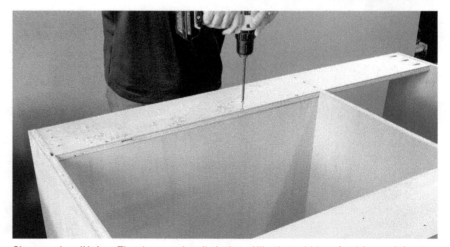

Clamp rack wall is key. The clamp rack wall, designed like the webbing of an I-beam, is key to the cart's design, and functions to prevent both racking and sagging. Reinforce the connection to prevent both racking and sagging. Reinforce the connection to the cleat strip with glue and 1 ½"-long #8 screws.

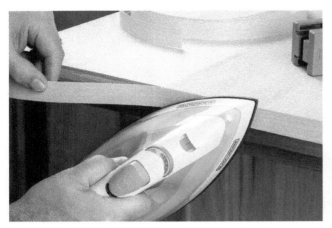

Add edge banding. Cover any exposed edges with maple edge banding. I use the iron-on variety, and align one edge to the plywood veneer as I go. The opposite edge overhangs the plywood, and will be trimmed off later.

Cut clamp rack. Plane a board to fit the dado, and cut a series of notches with a ½"-wide dado stack. Crosscut the clamp rack to fit, and glue it in the shallow dado.

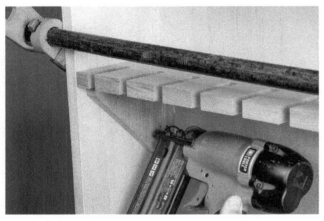

Add supports. Attach three small triangular supports with glue and fasteners. Now your clamp rack is complete and ready for years of service.

Dovetails by jig. A variable-spaced dovetail jig and router make quick work of the standard through-dovetail corners. A dovetail bit handles the tails, while a straight bit cuts the pins.

Draw front cut-outs. One template handles both shapes. Adhere the template to your workpiece with double-sided carpet tape and clamp them to a workbench (left). Trim to final shape (right).

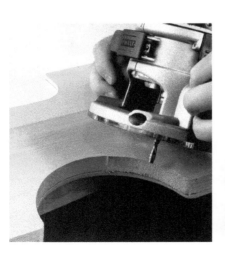

from the top and attached to each end panel with pocket hole screws.

WHEELS AND CLAMP RACK

Before the cart gets too heavy, turn it upside down and add 4" locking casters at each corner. Finish the carcase by adding maple edge banding to any exposed edges. I used iron-on edge-banding and trimmed it flush once it cooled down. Take a moment to sand any sharp edges, and add the last fixed part to the base, a hardwood clamp rack. Use a ½" wide dado stack to cut evenly spaced notches in a 29 ¾"-long x 5 ½"-wide board.

The clamp rack is installed in a ¼"-deep dado in the clamp wall panel. Three small brackets offer additional support to the clamp rack. I sized mine for small parallel clamps; however, it could be adapted for various clamps in your shop. It's a handy spot to always have a clamp at the ready when assembling projects.

MAKING DRAWERS

I knew the drawers on this cart would carry a heavy load, and wanted them to last a lifetime, so I built them with solid hardwood lumber. The drawer boxes feature maple sides and walnut front and rear panels. The drawer bottoms are plywood panels. I used ¼" aromatic cedar plywood for the small top drawer, and more substantial ½" maple plywood for the lower two drawers. The corners are joined with through dovetail joinery, and were cut with a variable spacing dovetail jig.

Once the drawer boxes are built, install the full-extension drawer slides in the cabinet. Hang the drawers and test them for proper

CUT LIST & MATERIALS

	NO.	ITEM	T	W	L	MATERIAL
CARCASE						
☐	1	Worktop*	2	36 ½	56 ½	MDF
☐	1	Bottom panel	¾	30	49 ½	Maple plywood
☐	2	End panels	¾	30	31 ¾	Maple plywood
☐	1	Middle divider	¾	30	31 ¼	Maple plywood
☐	2	Top strips	¾	6	49 ½	Maple plywood
☐	1	White laminate		37	57	Plastic
☐	1	Worktop trim	¾	2	16'	Maple
☐	1	Iron-on edge banding		⅞	50'	Maple
☐	4	Locking swivel casters	4 dia.			
CLAMP RACK						
☐	1	Clamp rack wall	¾	30 ¼	30 ¼	Maple plywood
☐	1	Clamp rack component	¾	5 ½	29 ¾	Maple plywood
☐	3	Clamp rack brackets	¾	3	3	Maple plywood
PASS-THROUGH SHELVES						
☐	2	Door panels	½	16 ¼	28 ⅜	Maple
☐	4	Door stiles	¾	1 ¾	31 ⅜	Maple plywood
☐	2	Upper door rails	¾	1 ¾	17 ¼	Maple plywood
☐	2	Lower door rails	¾	2 ¼	17 ¼	Maple plywood
☐	2	Pass-through shelves	¾	18	30	Maple plywood
☐	12	Shelf pins				
☐	2	3mm overlay cup hinge pairs				
DRAWERS						
☐	1	Top drawer false front	¾	6 ⁷⁄₁₆	30 ⅝	Maple
☐	2	Top drawer front and back	¾	5	28 ¾	Walnut
☐	2	Top drawer sides	¾	5	23 ½	Maple
☐	1	Top drawer bottom	¼	22 ¾	28	Cedar plywood
☐	1	Middle drawer false front	¾	12	30 ⅝	Maple
☐	1	Bottom drawer false front	¾	13	30 ⅝	Maple
☐	4	Lower drawer fronts and backs	¾	11	28 ¾	Walnut
☐	4	Lower drawer sides	¾	11	23 ½	Maple
☐	2	Lower drawer bottoms	½	22 ¾	28	Maple plywood
☐	3	Full-extension drawer slide pairs				

* Worktop is glued-up from one rectangle of 1" MDF with strips of the remaining sheet pieced together over top. MDF is then covered with plastic laminate.

operation. The finishing touch is the maple applied drawer fronts with curved cutouts. Mark the semicircular shapes for the drawer pulls, and joinery-exposing curves on each side.

Door rail tenons. With a sanding block or shoulder plane, shave the door rail tenons until they nestle into their mortises. Take light cuts and check the fit frequently for best results.

Haunched tenons. The 1" long x ¼" deep tenons are haunched to fit the door stiles (left). The extra tenon length adds strength to the joint (right).

Rough-cut the shapes at the bandsaw, and finish the job with a router and template setup. I made a two-sided template from a scrap of ¼" MDF to handle both shapes (see photos on p. 118, or make your own shape). Attach the template to the drawer with double-sided carpet tape, and chuck a bearing-guided flush-trimming bit in your router. Once the final trimming is done, ease the edges with a ⅛" radius roundover bit.

PASS-THROUGH DOORS

One limitation with typical shop cabinets is lack of space for long and bulky items. I wanted space to store my dovetail jigs and dowel stock, so I designed the cart with a pass-through cavity. It features long shelves that are accessible by a door on either side of the assembly table.

Build the doors with simple mortise-and-tenon construction, but make the tenons extra long for improved strength. The door is a solid maple panel, rabbeted to a ¼" tongue. If you're running low on hardwoods, ½" maple plywood is a reasonable substitute. Attach each door to the cart with a pair of overlay cup hinges. Cut two long shelves to fit, and install them on six shelf pins each.

EXTRA-THICK TOP

The top work surface is built-up from two layers of 1" thick MDF. Cut a piece of thick MDF 56 ½" x 36 ½", and use the rest of the sheet to make 8" and 12" wide strips. Attach the strips around the perimeter of the worktop, as well as over the carcase dividers. This stiffens the countertop, as well as achieves adequate bearing on the cabinet framework. Instead of try-

LAYOUT: PLYWOOD CUTTING

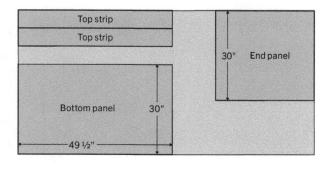

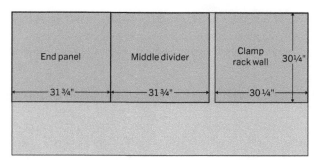

LAYOUT: MDF CUTTING

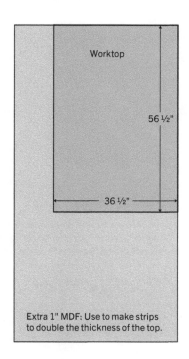

Extra 1" MDF: Use to make strips to double the thickness of the top.

EXPLODED VIEW: CARCASE

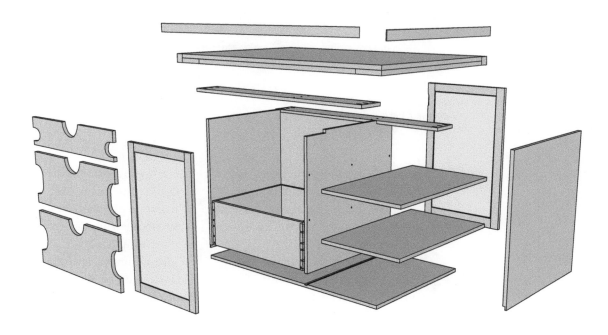

Drawer gap. Use a spacer stick to set the 1/16" gap between drawers, and attach the drawer fronts with carpet tape. Permanently secure the drawer front with five screws driven from inside the drawer box.

Door cutouts. No metal knobs here, which could interfere with clamps when the cart is in use. Instead, a cove cut that aligns with the top drawer cutout makes a convenient finger pull to open the door.

Laminate top. Attach a durable laminate surface to the thick MDF top with contact cement. Once the contact cement tacks over, press the laminate firmly in place with a J-roller or workpiece support roller.

Flush. Install a laminate trimming bit in a compact router, and trim the surface flush.

ing to align the edges perfectly, let the strips overhang the top panel slightly. Attach the strips with glue and screws, and flush trim the edges once the glue dries.

Now add plastic laminate, for a work surface that's durable and easy to clean. Apply contact cement to both surfaces with a low-nap paint roller and allow it to tack over until it feels dry to the touch. The paint rollers for smooth walls with a 1/8" or 1/4" nap seem to work best. Apply the laminate, allowing it to overhang the top in all directions.

With a trim router and laminate trimming bit, flush up the plastic laminate around the edges. Use a J-roller, or top half of a shop workpiece support roller, to press the

Shelf pins. Install six shelf pins per shelf, and trace the location of each one. Then cut shallow recesses with a router (left), before dropping the shelf in place (right).

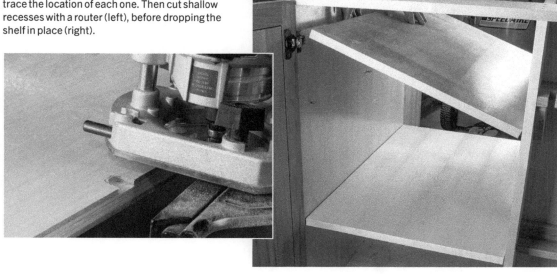

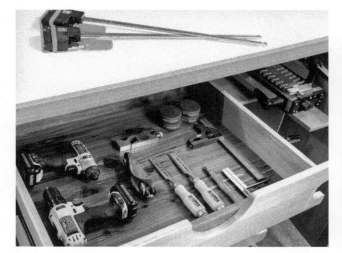

Load 'em up. Load the drawers with your most frequently used tools, and they'll be within reach on your next project.

Oversized drawers. Even bulky routers stored upright will disappear. Just like the cabinet doors, skip metal drawer pulls for unfettered access when clamping workpieces to your table.

laminate firmly to the substrate. The final step to complete the top is to add hardwood trim around the edges. I dressed the top out with 2" wide x ¾" thick maple boards, mitered to fit. The maple edging is attached with biscuits and glue and clamped in place.

Applying finish is optional, but I like to add a few coats of something for a bit of protection—usually whatever I have on hand. This assembly table is finished with water-based polyurethane, which I've used on a lot of my shop furniture. It's simple to apply and makes things easy to clean up. All that's left to do is load it up and start working. ∎

THE MILKMAN'S WORKBENCH

This full-featured benchtop clamps to any solid surface.

BY CHRISTOPHER SCHWARZ

One of the best things about working with hand tools is you don't need much shop space—often a corner of a bedroom provides enough space. And a complete tool kit fits in a box the size of blanket chest.

As a result, many apartment-dwellers work with hand tools because they are compact, relatively quiet, and fairly easy to clean up after. But there is one huge thing missing from the above—a good workbench.

Woodworking is much easier with a solid workbench that is equipped with vises and bench dogs. Good workbenches are usually massive and enormous, and they might not fit in tight quarters. A big bench can also be intimidating to build for a beginning woodworker. And small commercial benches are generally too spindly for real woodwork.

Enter the Milkman's Workbench—a small, full-featured benchtop that clamps to any solid surface—a dining table, dresser, or kitchen island. And it's not just for the apartment-dweller. This is a great bench for traveling, demonstrating at woodworking clubs, or even for working in the living space of your home if you have a shop without HVAC.

It offers a lot of features for such a small thing. You can dovetail boards more than 19" wide in its twin-screw vise area. You can pinch boards almost 24" long between dogs, and you have a decent work surface for chopping. Best of all, you can attach it to something sturdy using only two F-style clamps, do your business, then put the bench away in a closet or under a bed.

I first saw a commercial version of this bench on an Australian auction site. At that time, I had a student, Jonas Jensen, whose father owned one. He had bought it from the town's milkman. I purchased the original from Jonas' father, studied its construction, and worked with it for months. I concluded it was nearly perfect.

This version is almost identical to the original, with only slight changes to make it easier to clamp to your work surface.

Essential grooves. Before you do any assembly, cut the grooves for the wagon vise.

Digging for dogs. Cutting the dog holes using a dado stack makes for crisp work.

Snouts for dogs. These notches allow the dogs to rest below the benchtop when not in use.

DETAIL: VISE BLOCK

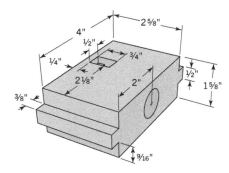

DETAIL: DOG HOLES, MIDDLE BENCHTOP

3D VIEW

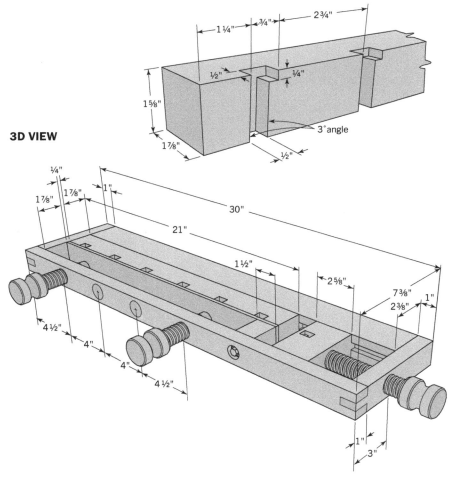

CONSTRUCTION OVERVIEW

There's little joinery in this bench. The corners of the frame are joined by bridle joints that are pinned with ⅜" dowels. The frame is screwed to the benchtop it surrounds. The benchtop is just glued together with edge joints.

The only tricky part of the bench is the wagon vise. It's a block of wood that slides in two grooves plowed into the internal surfaces of the bench.

All the vises are powered by 1¼"-diameter threaded wooden screws, which I made with a lathe and a threading kit from Beall Tool Co. (see "Make Threaded Wooden Screws" on p. 128 for details on the system). You don't have to invest in a threading system to make this bench: You can purchase three veneer-press screws and use those instead. You can also simplify by installing round dogs instead of square ones.

The place to begin your bench is at the lumberyard.

STABLE, DRY, AND STRAIGHT

The original bench looks to be made of beech. Because beech is hard to come by in the Midwest, I opted for red maple, though almost any wood will do. What is more important than the species is that the grain is straight, the stock is dry, and there isn't a lot of internal stress in the wood.

I purchased about 8 board feet of 8/4 maple for the bench.

Using my cutting list, I milled all the stock close to size—1" overlong and ¼" overwide. As I progressed through the project, I brought the pieces I needed to final size.

ASSEMBLE THE MIDDLE

The benchtop inside the frame has three significant pieces: the rear benchtop, the middle benchtop, and a thin strip that covers the dog holes. Before you can glue the rear and middle benchtop together, you need to plow a stopped groove in the rear benchtop for the wagon vise. This groove is ½" wide x ⅜" deep x 7" long. It's centered in the thickness of the rear benchtop. After you cut this groove, cut a similar groove—but 8" long—in the front frame. That's the other groove for the wagon vise.

Glue the rear and middle benchtop pieces together. When the glue is dry, level the seams, then lay out the location of the ½" x ½" dog holes on the front edge of this assembly. You can cut these by hand with a backsaw and router plane, or you can use a dado stack in your table saw.

Whichever way you go, it's best to cut the dog holes so they are angled about 3°. They need to lean toward the wagon vise—this helps the dog pinch your work against the benchtop.

With the dog holes cut, you need to make a notch at the top of each hole for the snout of the dog. The notch is ¼" x ½" x ¼" deep. Chop out the notch with a chisel and finish the floor with a router plane.

Then glue the ¼"-thick strip over the front edge of your benchtop. When the glue is dry, level the seams and square up the ends of the benchtop. You are ready to make the frame.

THE FRAME: BRIDLES AND SCREWS

Cut your frame pieces to their final lengths by using the assembled benchtop as a guide. Then cut the bridle joints at the corners. Note that the "slot" half of the bridle joint has to be cut on the front piece of the frame. Otherwise, the groove you already milled for the wagon vise shows.

After the bridle joints are cut and the frame wraps around the three sides of the benchtop, you should bore the four holes for the movable vise screws in the front piece of the frame and the end piece where your wagon vise is located. If you are using a 1¼" threading kit (such as Beall), you'll need to bore 1⅛"-diameter holes. Use the drawings to lay out their location. Bore all the holes, then tap them for the threads.

Next you need to cut the spacer block that holds the frame away from the benchtop, making room for your

Tap the holes. A simple pair of locking pliers can help you turn the tap into the holes in the frame.

	NO.	ITEM	DIMENSIONS (INCHES)			MATERIAL
			T	W	L	
☐	1	Rear benchtop	1⅝	2⅜	28	Maple*
☐	1	Middle benchtop	1⅝	1⅞	21	Maple
☐	1	Dog hole cover strip	¼	1⅝	21	Maple
☐	1	Front frame	1⅝	1	30	Maple
☐	2	Frame ends	1⅝	1	7⅜	Maple
☐		Joint pegs	⅜ dia.			Dowel
☐	1	Spacer block	1⅝	1½	1⅞	Maple
☐	1	Vise block	1⅝	2⅝	4¾	Maple
☐	1	Garter	¼	1⅝	2	Maple
☐	3	Vise hubs	1¾-dia.		2⅜	Maple
☐	2	Face vise rods	1¼-dia.		5†	Maple
☐	1	Wagon vise rod	1¼-dia.		7¾	Maple
☐	1	Lag screw and washer	⅜		4	Maple
☐		Clamping mounts			2	Angle iron
☐		Bench dogs				Maple

CUT LIST & MATERIALS

* Any seasoned, straight-grained wood will do; † Trim to fit vise block.

MAKE THREADED WOODEN SCREWS

Wooden vise screws are quite durable (as long as you don't abuse them). Once you have a rig to make them, you'll be eager to make your own hand screws, panel clamps, and other useful shop gizmos.

Sadly, the modern manual wood-threading kits are fragile and fussy—I've burned through four sets. So when it comes to making precise, clean threads, the best method is the Beall Tool Co. wood-threading system.

This American-made and patented system uses a router-powered threader to create the threads. The tap is hand-powered, but it uses an ingenious pilot bearing to ensure you tap holes dead straight.

The instructions and enclosed DVD are quite good, but here are some tips that aren't covered.

1. Precise and sturdy stock is imperative. Home-center dowels don't work, but hardwoods with tight, straight grains work best. Turn your own (I did) or buy some tight-tolerance dowels from Beall.

2. Soaking the dowels in alcohol or linseed oil overnight makes for cleaner threads.

3. Despite what the DVD shows, don't back out your threaded rods from the jig while the router is running.

4. Longer lengths of dowel are better than short lengths. Threading 12" lengths (at minimum) is best.

5. The depth of the cut on the router is critical. A few thousandths of an inch makes an enormous difference in the shape of your threads.

6. Test every screw in a tapped sample hole before you commit to using it.

Here's how I made the vise screws for this bench. I sawed some straight stock into 1 3/8" octagons. I turned down the octagons into 1 1/4"-diameter cylinders. I turned them just a few thou shy of 1 1/4". Then I cut the threads on these dowels with the Beall system.

I chucked the dowels back in my lathe and turned 1"-diameter tenons on the ends of the dowels. I crosscut the threaded rods to the desired length.

Then I turned the hubs on my lathe from 1 3/4" stock. When the hubs were complete, I bored 1"-diameter holes to receive the tenons. I glued the threaded rods to the hubs using epoxy.

Make clean threads. The Beall system makes crisp threads, once you dial in the right settings and have some good stock to work with.

Turn with care. Turning the dowels slightly undersized pays off when cutting the threads.

Tenons on both ends. Here's the threaded dowel for the wagon vise. One end goes into the vise block, and the other into a hole in a hub.

Groove for a garter. Turn a 1/4"-wide x 1/8"-deep groove for the garter in the wagon vise.

Turn with more care. Keep the dowel moving into the jig steadily. Eventually, you will turn the dowel with one hand on the infeed side and one hand on the outfeed.

Hubs and screws. You can see how the hubs and threaded screws are assembled. The longer turned portion fits into the hub.

A close fit. The vise block needs to move smoothly. The less it wobbles in its grooves, the better.

Poke the block. Mark the centerpoint of the hole for the threaded screw using a Forstner bit. Layout is then almost foolproof.

Underside of block

Vise block. Here you can see the garter, the underside of the vise block, and the completed threaded screw.

face vise and your wagon vise. Cut two identical spacer blocks. One will be bolted in place permanently in your bench. The other will help you keep parts aligned as you assemble.

The best way to assemble the frame is to first attach the front piece and the end piece that does not house the wagon vise. Leave the other end piece unattached for now so you can fit the wagon vise.

The front part of the frame is bolted to the benchtop spacer block with a ⅜" x 4" lag screw (don't forget the washer). The end piece is glued and screwed to the benchtop with three #10 x 1¾" wood screws. Drill the clearance holes and counterbores for all the hardware. Glue the corner of the frame then clamp together the two frame pieces, spacer blocks, and the front of the frame.

When everything is where it should be, drill your pilot holes for your hardware. Drive in the three #10 screws. Use a socket wrench to install the lag screw. Let the glue dry, then level the joints and turn your attention to the wagon vise.

THE WAGON VISE

If you have never built a vise like this, some of the parts—a garter?—can be baffling. But the photos and drawings will help the words do their job.

Here's how it works: The vise block is pushed forward by the threaded screw. The end of the threaded screw sits in a blind hole in the vise block. So far, so good. Now, here's where people get confused.

If you want the threaded screw to also retract the vise block, you need to do two things. You need to cut a ¼"-wide x ⅛"-deep groove around the circumference of the end of the threaded screw. You also need to make a "garter"—it's a block of wood that fits in a mortise in the vise block and intersects the blind hole. The garter locks together the threaded screw and the vise block. The photos do a better job than words can.

But before you make the garter, you need to shape the vise block so it slides smoothly in the grooves in the bench. So cut stub tenons on the ends of the vise block. The block should fit without wobbling like a loose tooth,

Hold-downs. These 2"-long sections of angle iron are easily screwed to the benchtop and then clamped to any surface with F-style clamps.

but it should slide back and forth with fingertip pressure.

With the vise block fit and in place, clamp the still-loose end of the frame to the benchtop. Place a 1⅛" Forstner bit in the hole in the end and prick its center point on the vise block. Remove the vise block and drill a 1"-diameter x ⅞"-deep hole in the vise block, using the center point to guide you.

There are two more steps to complete the vise block. First, add a ½" x ½" dog hole. You can make this hole in a variety of ways—chop it out by hand, use a hollow-chisel mortiser or bore a round hole then square it up. Add the snout like you did for the other dog holes. Last, you need to chop the mortise for the garter. That mortise is ¼" wide x 1⅝" long x 1¼" deep. It is centered on the hole for the vise screw. And it's ¼" from the end of the vise block. Whew.

To complete the work on the vise block, you need to fit the garter into the mortise you just cut and fit it to the groove in the end of the threaded screw. Again, words are not the ideal medium for comprehending this three-dimensional construction.

When everything in the wagon vise moves smoothly, glue and screw the end to the benchtop. Peg the bridle joints with ⅜"-diameter dowels.

Now turn your attention to making the threaded screws and hubs (i.e., handles).

CLAMPING HARDWARE AND FINISH

The original bench had wooden clamps below the top that would allow you to attach the benchtop to a table or other stout surface. These clamps, however, were easily worn out and pulled out of their mountings.

After many experiments, I settled on attaching 2"-long sections of angle iron to the rear edge of the benchtop and at the end of the bench opposite the wagon vise. These little bits of metal allow you to clamp the benchtop to any surface with F-style clamps.

With the benchtop complete and functioning, take apart everything you can and prepare the surfaces for finishing. I use a finish that is equal parts varnish, boiled linseed oil, and low-odor mineral spirits. Wipe the finish on with a rag. Remove the excess with a dry rag. Two coats should be enough for a bench.

Make some wooden dogs to suit your dog holes. They are pieces of maple that are friction-fit into the holes. And get to work—in the kitchen, the bedroom, or anywhere else you can find a stout surface. ■

A BENCH FOR KIDS

Build a small workbench with full-sized features for a budding woodworker.

BY JAMEEL ABRAHAM

The bench is probably the most important item in the workshop.

Those are Charles H. Hayward's first words in his article "Fitting Up the Workshop: The Bench." As a woodworking vise manufacturer and bench maker, I couldn't agree more. Tons of ink has been spilled about workbenches, and I'm one of the guilty parties, so I won't bore you with design philosophy on this one. OK, maybe a little.

Like a pro. Building a bench for a kid gives them a huge boost of self-confidence.

Cash cache. A sliding-lid bank is a great first project for your kid. Especially when you drop $20 in the slot before they take it home.

First off, a little background on why I decided to make a kid's workbench in the first place—perhaps a bit ironic for a bachelor. I've lived next door to my brother for a number of years and have probably spent more time in the shop with my nieces and nephews than if I'd had my own kids. Relationships between parents and children aren't always conducive to teaching (I'm reminded of why the "Car Talk" guys recommend that parents not teach their own kids to drive). But trying to be the fun uncle placed me in a position to not only teach without the typical parent/child dynamics, but to make the workshop a fun environment instead of a stuffy classroom. In my experience, fun is the key element in teaching kids woodworking.

A few years ago, I decided to build a kid's workbench as a prize for a tool event. The idea was simple. Build the bench, have kids write their name on the edge of a piece of basswood held in the bench's leg vise, then plane off the shaving (along with their name) and place it in a box for a drawing the next day. The winner would take the bench home with them.

Dozens of kids participated, and it was great fun watching half of them completely ignore the piece in the vise and start planing the top of the bench itself! One young boy spent a long time at the bench and made many shavings (but only one with his name on it). I watched him several times, and it was apparent that he'd spent time in the shop. I was extremely busy both days of the event, and only found one moment to take some video of the kids planing away. It was this boy who I ended up recording and posting to social media. The next afternoon we had a young girl reach into the box of names and pull out one winner. Incredibly, out of dozens of names,

CUT LIST & MATERIALS

	NO.	ITEM	DIMENSIONS (INCHES)			MATERIAL
			T	W	L	
☐	1	Top	1¾	11⅝	43½	Yellow pine
☐	1	Apron	1¼	4½	45	Yellow pine
☐	1	Front stretcher	1¾	2¼	31½	Yellow pine
☐	2	Side stretchers	1¾	2¼	10¾	Yellow pine
☐	1	Rear stretcher	1¾	2¾	31½	Yellow pine
☐	2	Side rails	1¼	2¼	6½	Yellow pine
☐	1	Rear rail	1¼	2¾	41	Yellow pine
☐	2	Front legs	1½	2¼	22½	Yellow pine
☐	2	Rear legs	1½	2¼	23¾	Yellow pine
☐	1	Vise support	1	2¼	18	Hardwood
☐	1	Vise chop	1⅝	3⅛	24	Hardwood
☐	1	Tool well bottom	½	5¼	42	Yellow pine
☐	1	Rear edging	¾	1¾	43½	Yellow pine
☐	2	End edgings	¾	1¾	16½	Yellow pine
☐	*	Shelf boards	½	*	13¾	Yellow pine
☐	1	Plane stop cleat	1	2	4	Hardwood
☐	1	Plane stop	¼	4	12	Plywood

* Width and number of shelf boards can vary; cut to fit.

Grandpa's Workmate. The Black + Decker Workmate makes a great tester bench to see if your kid has that first spark of interest.

the winner was the same boy I had recorded the day before. I knew that this bench was going to a good home.

Designing the bench was rather easy. I'd flipped open my copy of the *The Woodworker, Volume 4* and there it was: a basic bench that would scale down perfectly. I'd built a few kid's benches over the years and I knew that it only needed a couple workholding features—a face vise and a planing stop. Kids don't need anything more than this. You could use any basic iron face vise, but I chose the Benchcrafted Hi Vise hardware.

Before you get too deep into building this bench, you might want to dust off an old Black + Decker Workmate and toss some softwoods on it

to see if your kid has some interest. I did this early on with the kids, and they were hooked. The Workmate can be set up at the perfect height for a young child, and the clamping capabilities are sufficient for that first dabble into the craft. It's not ideal, though, with its sharp metal edges and somewhat awkward layout, but there's no better hook than telling the kid that the next project is his or her own bench.

To get started, I drew all the major components in SketchUp right from Hayward's plan; using the scale feature, I made the height 24" and all the components scaled down just about perfectly. I've included a cutlist, model, and drawings of the bench, but don't be a slave to them. If you want to make a wider or narrower bench, simply make the rails between the front and back legs longer or shorter. If you're using a leg vise, double check that you have enough space between the front and back leg for the screw's length with the vise completely closed. The measurements I used here work with the Bench-crafted Hi Vise hardware.

All the components can be made from 8/4 stock. I used yellow pine from my hardwood lumber dealer, which comes with the full 8/4 thickness, but you could easily use 2x material from the home center. My legs and rails ended up being 1¾" thick. If using 2x material, 1⅜" would be fine after jointing and planing.

SIMPLE JOINERY

Once I had true stock to work with, it was time for joinery. And here was where I enlisted the help of my German friend, Mr. Domino. For full-size benches, I never skimp on joinery. I like to view workbenches as miniature timber frames—I want every bench I build or design to be in use for at least a couple hundred years. But for a kid's bench that won't ever see vigorous use, the Domino is just about the perfect joinery system. It's plenty strong enough, and the speed and ease of layout and cutting means you won't feel ridiculous as you might had you spent a week cutting through-wedged tenons. It doesn't take much more time to double up on the Dominos either, and it adds loads of glue surface and strength. If you don't have access to a Domino, you can of course build the bench with traditional joinery. I won't tell on you, I promise.

Cutting parts for a project with Domino joinery is straightforward. Just cut each of your legs, stretchers, and rails to final lengths. You don't need to add any length for tenons.

Marking the layout for Domino tenons is also easy. All you need is one tick mark spanning each joint

Go to detention. After ripping, this wood threw a temper tantrum and got bent out of shape, so I pushed it into a corner and let it cool off for a time out. A couple days and a second round of jointing and planing yielded flat stock.

Order and accuracy. Measure up the rail lengths by using a mock-up of the legs—the leg spacing is determined by your choice of bench width. The large square and bevel gauge position the legs perfectly for accurate measuring (left). The same technique is used to measure the length of the stretchers (right).

Don't go to recess. Try to sneak up on the correct length so the top surface of the rail ends up dead flush with the top of the legs. If it's too long or short, it will either be proud or recessed. I nibble away the length at the miter saw during my snack break.

You get an A+. Here are the two leg assemblies cut to final dimension and dry-fit without Domino tenons.

and away you go. If you've ever used a biscuit joiner, you can use a Domino. I set the fence on the machine for a double tenon centered on the thickness of the stretchers and rails, because they are the thinner members. I cut the first mortise (Domino slot) on all the workpieces, adjusted the fence, then cut all the lower mortises. That step took maybe 20 minutes. The Domino is so fast you'll think you're cheating, so make sure the teacher isn't watching.

Cutting the Domino mortises can be tricky on short and narrow pieces. Festool makes a special table for holding pieces like this. But so do I—it's called a workbench. Mine has a tail vise and bench dogs. I gang up on the little rascals and pinch their sides between the dogs. This gives more surface area for the fences of the Domino. The last thing you want is for your workpiece to jump over a fence during class, so doubling up on these is a good move. It also cuts your clamping time in half, leaving more time for after-school antics.

EXPLODED VIEW

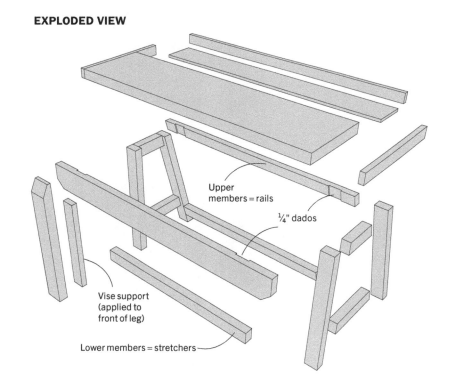

Upper
members = rails

¼" dados

Vise support
(applied to
front of leg)

Lower members = stretchers

Let's play Dominos. Here's the setup for cutting the mortises—quick and simple. A tail vise and dogs are handy here.

Dado no blado. I don't use a dado stack for the mortises because I'm too lazy to mount it. Instead, I take multiple passes with a combo blade, then clean up with a router plane.

Once the mortises are cut, it's a good idea to dry-fit every joint. Assemble the bench and make sure every joint goes together with all the Dominos in place (or your tenons, if you went the traditional route). Clamp the leg assemblies together

at the front stretcher to mark for the front apron. The front apron is joined to the upper part of the legs in a shallow dado cut into the back of the apron. Clamp the apron to the upper part of the legs and mark the location of the legs onto the back of the apron. The dado is only ¼" deep, so I cut it on the table saw by nibbling away the waste, then cleaned up the bottom of the dado with a router plane.

THE VISE

With the front apron joinery cut, you have a decision to make. Mount an off-the-shelf iron vise or install a leg vise, like I did. I'll talk about how to do the latter. Because the front apron is proud of the front leg by 1", I laminate a 1"-thick piece of hardwood onto the front leg below the apron. This provides a strong place to mount the pins that support the vise mechanism. The vise itself is contained entirely

FRONT VIEW

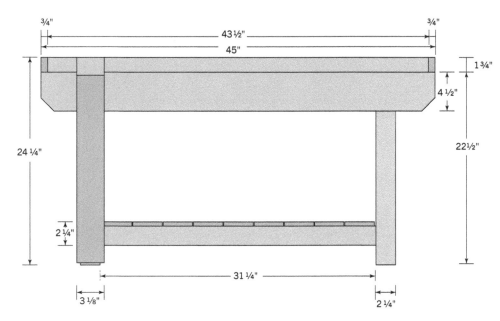

SIDE VIEW (CHOP AND VISE SUPPORT REMOVED)

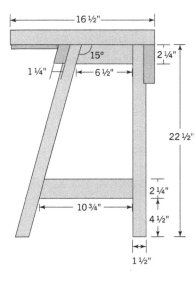

within the leg and chop, so the installation should be completed now, before gluing the bench together. I won't cover all the details of the vise installation here because you may not be using this specific vise.

Once you have the bench's top flattened and planed to thickness, you can dry-assemble the bench and get a final length for the vise chop. This allows you to disassemble the vise, cut the chop to length and do any decorative shaping as well.

FINISHING THE BUILD

To cut the top to length, mill up the stock that makes up the edging so you have a final thickness. You need this thickness because the top is shorter than the front apron by exactly twice the thickness of the edging. I don't measure any of this, so put your rulers away. Rather, hold up two thicknesses of edging to one end of the top (with the other end flush to the end of the apron) and mark the length.

With the top cut to length and width, you can glue the front of it to the apron. Make the joint as perfectly flush as you can, but err on the side of the top being proud of the apron. It will be much easier to flush the edge of the top to the apron rather than vice versa.

Now disassemble the dry-fit base to smooth-plane the surfaces. Don't go overboard here. You just want to remove the mill marks. If you've built the bench entirely by hand, well, you don't need any instruction from me on how to do this.

Now glue the base together. I use the offcuts from the angled rails as cauls between the clamps and the

Textures. Router planes are the greatest. They are like hand tool power tools, if that makes sense.

Vised up. Install the leg vise before you glue the bench together.

Transfer, don't measure. Here I'm marking the length of the top—the apron length minus two thicknesses of edging.

Caul me in the morning. Angled spacer blocks make leg assembly glue-up easy.

back legs. After the glue in the leg assemblies cures, glue and assemble the stretchers to the assemblies. Once the glue in the base is cured, rip the upper back rail with a 15° angle on the top side (and bottom, too, if you want; I didn't) and fit it up just like the front apron, with ¼"-deep dados. Glue and clamp, then flush it up to the top with a long plane.

Once the top is screwed to the base and the edging is attached, you can install the tool tray bottom. It's just a piece of ½"-thick pine nailed on from underneath. I used square-cut nails

Get it together. The top is held onto the base with lag screws. Use two in each upper rail. Make sure the front apron is clamped firmly to the legs when you drill and drive the lags.

Hammer time. Actually, it's glue time, but hammer time sounds cooler. Get that joint flush or you'll have loads of cleanup planing to do. I'm not gluing the top to the base here, just using it as a support.

Cleatus, repeatus. I clamp a cleat to the top on both ends to rest the edging on to measure its length, drill the screw holes, then attach it to the top. The cleat keeps everything lined up and helps you to not think too much.

with robust heads. I also leave a 2" gap at the leg-vise end of the well to sweep out shavings. The shelf boards down below are plain, nailed on with two finish nails in the center of each board, with a 1⁄16" gap between each board. The ends are notched to fit around the legs.

And just like that, class is over, the bell has rung, and the bench is done. If you want to paint the base and vise chop like I did, simply unscrew the top from the base and put a coat of oil on it, then apply two coats of paint on the base and chop. I like solid-color deck stain. It looks a lot like milk paint without any of the associated mixing and shelf life.

USING THE BENCH

To hold boards for edge work, just use the leg vise. To plane the faces of boards, also use the leg vise with a planing stop. To make the planing stop, screw a 1" x 2" hardwood cleat on edge to the short end of a ¼"-thick piece of plywood or hardwood that's about 4" wide x 12" long. Clamp the hardwood cleat in the leg vise with the longer board flat on the workbench, and it becomes a full-width planing stop. (The one shown at p.

139 is for a full-sized bench.) I don't recommend a metal-toothed stop for kids for obvious reasons. This full-width stop is user-friendly and will keep any board from moving about, while teaching good technique at the same time.

To hold boards for end work, use the leg vise or simply clamp boards

to the front apron and top with small clamps. You could also add holdfast holes, but that might be a little overkill for a kid's bench. The holes in the right leg are for supporting longer boards. Just stick a ¾" dowel in and it's ready to go. ■

Handscrew it. To bolster the rear edging, I handscrew it to the side edging. This helps keep the wood from splitting while screwing. Hayward says to nail these on, but I'm not Hayward the Magnificent. Nailing into end grain equals splits in my book. Big robust screws and properly sized pilot holes are wonderful things.

I have zero clout. So I try to buy it whenever I can. I use clout nails to attach the tool well bottom, laying out the spacing with a pair of big dividers. There's a nail about every 6".

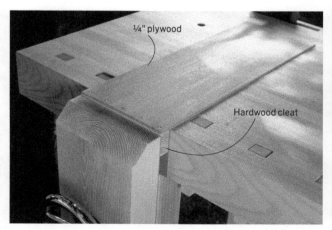

Just plane stop it. A planing stop can be made with two pieces of scrap. It's a great workbench accessory, and will teach good technique.

Bench bench, who's got the bench? I'm using four benches here to flatten the top of a bench, including the bench I'm flattening. Looks ridiculous, I know, but my back is happy.

2

ACCESSORIES

Now it's time to accessorize your workbench. Regardless of the design you choose, workbenches are only as useful as their ability to hold the piece you're working on. These creative work-holding solutions are simple enough to craft yourself. Dive in for instructions to create a bench hook, deadman, doe's foot, raamtang, and more. Combined with pegs, bench dogs, holdfasts, and face vises, you'll be able to securely hold any shape and size of workpiece on your new bench.

UPGRADE YOUR WORKBENCH

These simple and ingenious jigs will unlock the full capacity of your workbench.

BY ROB PORCARO

The most important tool in my shop is one I never pick up: the workbench. I purchased my bench years ago, a classic Continental-style model with a trestle base, a wooden face vise, and an end vise, with a row of square bench dog holes along the front of the work surface. Though it has served me well and I'd buy, or more likely make, the same style bench (bigger, of course) if I had to do it over again, I've made significant adaptations to it to get my work done efficiently. I don't consider this a shortcoming of the basic design. It only means that this tool can be personalized, just like almost all other tools, to meet the demands of one's work.

Problems arose in holding boards that were long or wide, and in managing thin, narrow strips of stock. The face vise would rack when tightened down with a board occupying one side of the jaw. I also needed a place for movable lighting without losing work surface. The heavy steel bench dogs proved to be overkill for almost all my work and were menaces to edge tools. I also needed, of course, accessories for shooting edges, trimming tenon shoulders, and assorted small trimming tasks.

The following bench modifications are easy to make and don't produce major irreversible scars to your bench or fight the time-honored basic design. The alterations use some modern materials, most notably aluminum T-track. While retaining great respect for designs evolved over centuries, we can continue to improve upon them.

Some basics first, however.

The height of my bench is adjusted with blocks screwed to the base to allow the heel of my hand to touch the benchtop with about a 135° bend at the elbow. I chose this criterion for height by trial and error in various bench tasks. A height of 35" works for me. Nonetheless, having an adjustable-height stool available has been a great help in relieving the strain of standing all the time.

A plywood shelf screwed to my stretchers is loaded with heavy items, such as a machinist's vise and a granite surface plate, to add at least 100 pounds to the bench. I also cov-

SIDE VIEW: TOGGLE CLAMP SLED

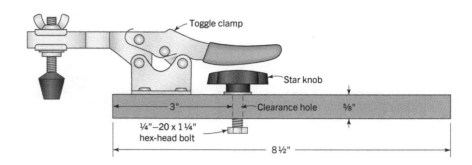

When your work is wide. Many benches struggle to secure wide stock so you can work on the ends. Some T-track, a toggle clamp, and a star knob can fix that problem.

ered the base where it contacts the floor with high-friction tape. Even on a varnished shop floor, the bench, while not massive in dimensions, is amazingly stable.

A word about the following jigs: not all projects shown have materials included in the cut list, because the sizes of the parts is relative to your particular bench and needs.

HOLD WIDE BOARDS IN YOUR FACE VISE
My toggle clamp sled allows me to secure a board of any width to work on its end grain, such as dovetailing. To make this jig, first install T-track into a groove routed in the front edge

For the long stuff. This jig clamps into my tail vise to help me hold long work. The toggle clamp sled slides in the T-track to adjust for different widths.

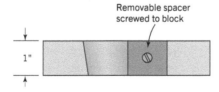

The jig in action. The crosspieces at the top of the jig keep it in place as I tighten the tail vise. Then, I just slide the toggle clamp sled in position.

of your benchtop. (It is helpful to handplane this front edge straight and square to the top.) A toggle-cam clamp is screwed to a sliding wooden carrier, which is set in place along the track with a standard ¼"-20 hex bolt and a plastic star knob. Leave some clearance at the end of the groove so the bolt head can enter the track.

To use the sled, secure a wide board on its left side with the jaw of the face vise and on its right side by the toggle clamp. This makes for a solid hold across the width of the board, keeps it flat, and greatly reduces vibration when sawing. This also works very well for holding a frame-and-panel door to trim its edges or ends.

WORK THE EDGES OF LONG BOARDS

To work the edges of long or wide boards, I made another jig that uses T-track and my toggle clamp sled. This jig clamps into my tail vise. To make this jig, install T-track into a 1½"-square by 26"-long piece of a

TOP VIEW: WEDGE VISE

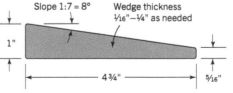

Removable spacer screwed to block

1"

SIDE VIEW: WEDGE VISE

Slope 1:7 = 8°   Wedge thickness ⅟₁₆"–¼" as needed

1"

4¾"   5⁄16"

FRONT VIEW: WEDGE VISE

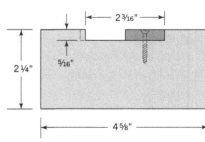

2³⁄₁₆"

5⁄16"

2¼"

4⅝"

The wedge vise in use. One of the beauties of this jig is that the more you push on the work, the tighter it is secured in the jig.

The vise and its wedges. Here's the jig before it goes into the tail vise. The different wedges are used for workpieces of different thicknesses.

dense hardwood (I used bubinga). Screw in crosspieces at the top (left photo, p. 144) to easily and securely fit the jig into the tail vise. The sliding toggle-clamp carrier is inserted into the track and can be adjusted to support the bottom edge of a long/ wide board whose other end is held in the face vise. Tightening the toggle clamp then prevents lateral movement and vibration of the long board.

Add mounts for swing lamps. These blocks are notched into the tool tray of my bench. The bronze sleeve accepts the post of a swing-arm lamp.

Make as many as you need. Position these brackets at a few points around your benchtop and purchase one quality swing-arm lamp. Then just move the lamp wherever you need light.

WEDGE VISE HOLDS SMALL PIECES

Working on thin or narrow stock can be difficult, and that's when I turn to my wedge vise. This jig is a 1" x 4 5/8" x 2 1/4" block with a 5/16"-deep recess in the top, angled 1:7 on one side. I clamp it in my tail vise with some of the recess proud of the top surface of the bench. Then I tap a wedge of appropriate thickness into place to secure pieces that are thin, narrow, or small. These pieces can be otherwise difficult to hold or may move when planed against a simple end stop. The

photo at top right shows a narrow, thin, long piece of mahogany solidly held in this device. Note the removable spacer, secured by a single screw, which allows for a range of workpiece widths.

SIMPLE LAMP BRACKETS

Bubinga has great shear strength. Screw blocks of it into recesses at each side of the bench. A hole in the block holds a sintered bronze sleeve bushing, length and diameter to match your lamp. Drive a small screw

Better bench dogs. The wooden springs on these dogs allow you to use them in high or low positions with ease. The replaceable faces keep me from having to make lots of these dogs.

Handplane runs on its side here.

Traditional shooting board. This shooting board is clamped between dogs on my benchtop. It can be used for trimming edge grain or end grain with a handplane.

Red lines remind you of screws.

Bench hook with extra grip. When trimming the shoulders of tenons, I like to have my work well-secured. The toggle clamp on this jig will hold my stock while I work the joint with a shoulder plane.

in from the side of the block and let the tip bite into the bronze to prevent the bushing from being lifted from the block when the lamp is moved. These brackets allow instant relocation of a commonly available articulating office lamp. The lamp is well supported and rotates freely. These brackets have worked well for more than 15 years without replacement or wear.

SPRING-LOADED DOGS

The wooden springs (typically at a 3° angle) make my bench dogs height-adjustable. The top cross section is just small enough to allow the dog to be buried below the benchtop when desired. The softwood bearing face can be chiseled off every once in a long while when it gets worn and a new one glued on.

SHOOTING BOARD

The 6"-wide quartersawn mahogany top, with slots for solid wood movement, is screwed to a 9"-wide MDF base; both parts are 26" long. The 3"-wide surface on which the planes rides is covered with ⅛" adhesive-backed UHMW plastic. The end-grain stop is easily modified or replaced, and the edge of the solid wood top can also be easily dressed as the shooting board is "broken in."

BENCH HOOK WITH A CLAMP

A cleat below the jig (not shown) holds the device in the tail vise; a toggle clamp quickly secures the work leaving hands free for planing. Overall dimensions are 15" x 9". I use this hook a lot for trimming tenon shoulders. The tenon shoulder butts against the stop, which is secured

For pushing and pulling. By placing the stop in the middle of the bench hook I can use it with both Western and Japanese saws.

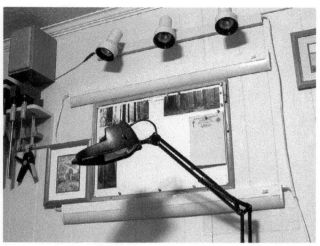

Different lights for different jobs. I have a variety of directional and non-directional lights in my shop so I can turn things on and off until I achieve the result I need to see my work.

to the main fence with safely counterbored screws. The red lines are a reminder of the presence and depth of the screws. For instructions on making your own bench hook, see page 178.

BENCH HOOK FOR BOTH WESTERN AND EASTERN HANDSAWS

Nothing fancy here. The stop placed in the middle allows the use of both push- and pull-stroke saws. This also gets plenty of use with chiseling tasks on small pieces.

ADDITIONAL LIGHTING

Bright track lights, two levels of fluorescent lights, and an articulating office lamp are used to produce the angle, brightness, and color rendition needed for various tasks.

I seek a sense of ease at the bench. That's what these jigs and upgrades are all about. ■

	NO.	ITEM	DIMENSIONS (INCHES)			MATERIAL
			T	W	L	
CUT LIST & MATERIALS						
TOGGLE CLAMP SLED						
☐	1	T-track	³⁄₈	³⁄₄	48	Aluminum
☐	1	Female wing knob	¹⁄₄–20		2	
☐	1	Hex-head bolt	¹⁄₄–20		1¹⁄₄	
☐	1	Low-silhoutte toggle clamp	¹⁄₄	2³⁄₄		
☐	1	Sliding carrier	⁵⁄₈	3	8¹⁄₂	Bubinga
LONG BOARD JIG						
☐	1	T-track	³⁄₈	³⁄₄	48	Aluminum
☐	1	Hardwood arm	1¹⁄₂	1¹⁄₂	26	Bubinga
☐	1	Bottom cross piece	1¹⁄₂	1¹⁄₂	4	Bubinga
☐	1	Top cross piece	¹⁄₂	2	3	Bubinga
WEDGE VISE						
☐	1	Jig block	1	4⁵⁄₈	2¹⁄₄	
☐		Wedges	*	1	4¹⁄₂	
SHOOTING BOARD						
☐	1	Top	³⁄₄	6	26	Quartersawn mahogany
☐	1	Base	³⁄₄	9	26	MDF
☐	1	Plane surface	¹⁄₈	3	26	Adhesive-backed UHMW plastic
☐	1	End-grain stop	³⁄₄	2	6	Mahogany

* Match measurements of workpiece to be clamped.

WORKBENCH ENRICHMENT

Here are ten ways to make your bench indispensable.

BY ROB PORCARO

I hate to say it, but no matter how much time and money you spent building or buying your work-bench, it's probably not as useful as it should be. Like adjustments to a new table saw or handplane, there are a number of things everyone should do to tune up their bench. Also, there are several simple improvements that will make your bench perform feats you didn't think were possible. Most of these upgrades are quick and inexpensive. All of them will make your woodworking easier, more accurate, or just plain tidier. Note that most don't require specific materials.

1. IMPROVE YOUR TOPOGRAPHY

Flattening your benchtop regularly is like changing the oil in your car. It's a routine step that will save you headaches down the road. A flat top is essential to accurate work for three reasons:

■ When planing, sanding, or routing a board, you want your work to rest firmly against your bench; a flat benchtop helps keep your work in place.

■ A flat top will divine whether your workpieces are cupped or bowed. If you ever want to remove the cup or twist from a door panel—a common malady—you must have a flat benchtop to know when your panel is finally flat.

■ A flat top guides you as you assemble your projects. If you want your latest table, chair, or cabinet to not rock, you have to make the legs or base all in the same plane. A flat bench will quickly point out your problems and the best solution.

So—how do you flatten a benchtop? The simplest way is to run it through a big drum sander, which you can find in mid-sized cabinet shops. The only downside is that you'll have some sanding grit embedded in your bench when it's all over, which can scratch your work in the future.

There is a way to flatten your bench at home by planing it with a router—once you build a somewhat complex carriage system that guides and holds the tool.

My way is faster. I flatten my benches with a No. 5 jack plane, an old No. 7 jointer plane, and a couple of sticks. The sticks are two pieces of plywood that measure ¾" x 2" x 36".

Traditionally called "winding sticks," these will quickly determine if your bench is flat and where it's out of whack.

First, place one of the winding sticks across one end of the bench. Lay the other stick across the bench at various places along the length of the top. Crouch down so your eye is level with the sticks to see if their top edges are parallel. If they are, that

Painted winding stick

Unpainted winding stick

Unwind. Winding sticks are the key to making sure a benchtop or tabletop is indeed flat. Check the top by moving the light-colored stick to different positions across the length of the bench and comparing the top edge of each stick.

Start on the sides. Most of the hard work when flattening your top is handled by the No. 5 jack plane, which can take down high spots quickly. My bench always seems to dish in the middle (similar to a waterstone), so I begin by taking down the sides.

PHOTOS BY AL PARRISH

Smooth it over. A No. 7 jointer plane's key asset is its length. Because of its length, the plane rides over the low spots and shears the high spots. Begin by working diagonally; don't worry about tear out (left). When the top is flat from your diagonal passes, plane directly with the grain (right).

area is flat. If they're not, you'll see where there are high spots.

Old-time winding sticks were made using a stable wood, such as mahogany, and were sometimes inlaid with ebony and holly on the edges (a black wood and a white wood) so you could easily see the difference. I prefer plywood because it's dimensionally stable and cheap. If you need contrast between your sticks, I highly recommend "ebony in a can" (i.e., black spray paint).

Mark all the high spots directly on your bench and start shaving them down with your jack plane. Continually check your work with your winding sticks. (For more on these sticks, see "Keep Your Winding Sticks in Focus" below.)

When the top is reasonably flat, fetch your No. 7 plane. First, plane the top diagonally, moving from corner to corner. Then, come back diagonally the other way. Do this a couple times until you're taking shavings at all points across the top. Finally, plane the length of the bench. Start at the front edge and move to the back edge. When it looks good, check it with the winding sticks.

2. A DEADMAN LENDS A HAND

One of the trickiest operations is working on the narrow edge of a board or door. Securing the work is the number one problem. The traditional solution is a sliding deadman. I installed the one shown here in an afternoon (see p. 156) and now I wonder how I ever got by without it.

Because the deadman slides across the front of the bench, you can accommodate all lengths of work. And, because the ledge can be adjusted up and down, you can hold narrow boards or even entryway doors. With the help of your face vise, you can immobilize almost anything with this rig.

I added the deadman by screwing two rails to my bench that each have a groove milled in one long edge. The deadman itself has a slightly undersized tenon on each end that allows it to slide in the grooves. For instructions on making your own deadman, see page 156.

TIP: KEEP YOUR WINDING STICKS IN FOCUS

When using winding sticks, one of the difficulties is trying to keep both sticks in focus when they are 6' away from each other. If one of the sticks is blurry, it's difficult to tell if they are in line with each other.

The solution comes from the world of photography. Take a piece of thin cardboard—I use the stuff from the back of a notebook. With your brad awl, punch a small hole (1/32" or so) in the center of the cardboard. Crouch down in front of your winding sticks and look at them through the hole. They should both be in focus.

In a camera, when you close the aperture (also called the F-stop), more of the picture is in focus. The same principle works with your eye. If you close the aperture that light passes through, more of what you see will be in focus.

As a practical matter when doing this, check both ends of the sticks by moving your eye left to right, not your head. It's easier to get a reading on your sticks this way.

3. ADD A LEG OR BENCH JACK

While I consider the sliding deadman to be the cat's meow, there are simpler ways to support oversized work at your bench.

If you do a lot of work on big doors, a leg jack is probably the best bet for you. Bore ¾"-diameter holes every 4" up the front leg of your bench that's opposite your face vise. (For example, if your vise is on the left side of your bench, bore the holes in the right leg.) Chamfer the holes (see the next section on dog holes for directions), then insert a ¾"-diameter dowel in one of the holes. You're in business.

The disadvantage of this jack is that it supports only long work. To hold shorter work, you need to add a second kind of jack to your bench—a bench jack.

For your bench jack, you'll bore the ¾"-diameter holes across the front edge of your workbench— every 4" or so should be sufficient. Make the holes about 2" deep and chamfer their rims.

Get a 2" length of ¾" dowel. To create a ledge for the board to rest on, your best bet is to buy an L-shaped piece of steel from your local hardware store. This item usually has screw holes already bored in it and is used for reinforcing corners.

Screw this L-shaped steel to the end of the dowel (see photo at right). This jig now will allow you to hold narrow boards of almost any length in place so you can safely work on the edge.

4. ADD BENCH DOGS

A good system of bench dogs and dog holes makes routine operations easier and impossible tasks a cake walk.

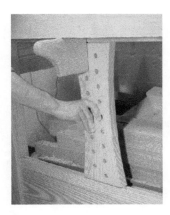

Deadman. While flattening the top is the most important upgrade, a close second is the sliding deadman. This clever bit of engineering will allow you to immobilize doors easily.

Leg jack

Leg jack. A leg jack is great for clamping long work, and it takes only about 20 minutes to add to your bench. There are fancier ways to do this, but none is more effective.

Bench jack

Bench jack. This simple bench jack excels at clamping boards that are 8" wide or narrower. Like the leg jack, this is a quick upgrade.

A pack of dogs. If you can't afford a tail vise, these adjustable clamp dogs make many clamping chores easier.

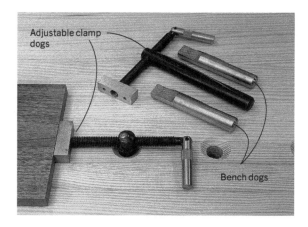

Adjustable clamp dogs

Bench dogs

round or other irregularly shaped pieces for sanding or planing.

To drill the dog holes, your best bet is to make a jig like the one shown below. Also, grab a ¾" auger bit and a corded drill.

Clamp the jig to your bench and drill the hole all the way through the benchtop. Use a slow speed. After you drill each hole, you need to chamfer the rim to keep from ripping up your benchtop when you pull out a dog. The easiest way to do this is with a plunge router.

Chuck a 45° chamfer bit that has a ¾" bearing on its end in your plunge router. Insert the bearing into the dog hole, turn on the router, and plunge straight down, making a ⅜"-deep cut.

Retrofitting a bench with round dog holes is quick and simple.

I like to have at least two rows of dog holes running down my benchtop that are spaced 4" apart. On some benches, I've had the dog holes line up with the dogs on my tail vise so that I can clamp things between my tail vise and any dog hole on the bench. But even if you don't have a tail vise, you can unlock the power of the dog hole with an adjustable clamp bench dog, such as a Wonder Dog. This is essentially a mini-vise that slips into any ¾"-diameter dog hole. It allows you to apply pressure in any direction, which is great for clamping

5. ADD A TAIL VISE

If you've got just one vise, it's almost always on the front (sometimes called the face) of your bench. A tail vise (located on the end of the bench) is an extremely useful upgrade. The retractable metal dog on most vises allows you to clamp really long workpieces to your bench between the vise's dog and a dog in the

Drill dog holes (left). This gizmo works like a primitive doweling jig. Mark lines on your top where you want your dog holes. Clamp this jig to your bench and line it up with your marks. Drill away using a corded drill. Chances are you'll cook a cordless drill.

An extra detail (right). Chamfering your dog holes prevents you from tearing out the grain when you remove a stubborn dog.

benchtop. It's also just plain handy to have a second vise.

When choosing a tail vise, you have three good options:

■ You can buy a reasonably priced traditional quick-release metal vise with a retractable dog that's easy to install.

■ You can buy a front-vise screw kit that you just add wooden jaws to. This option can be a bit cheaper, but requires more labor. The advantage to this vise is that you can add dog holes to the top or front edge of the wooden vise faces.

■ You can buy an expensive specialty vise that will do things your face vise won't. A twin-screw vise gives you a huge tail vise that can be used for clamping or holding almost any flat work. Or you can buy a patternmaker's vise that excels at holding irregular objects at any angle. Both of these are expensive, but worth it.

6. ADD A PLANING AND SANDING STOP

Many woodworkers clamp their work down when they don't have to. In many cases, gravity and the force of your tool will do the job.

A planing stop is essentially a lip on the end of your bench that can be adjusted up and down. When you're going to plane your work, you merely put the wood against the stop and plane into it. The force of gravity plus the direction in which you are pushing your tool holds the work in place.

The same concept works for belt sanding. Just remember which way the sander spins. The front of the sander should point away from the stop. Otherwise the machine will

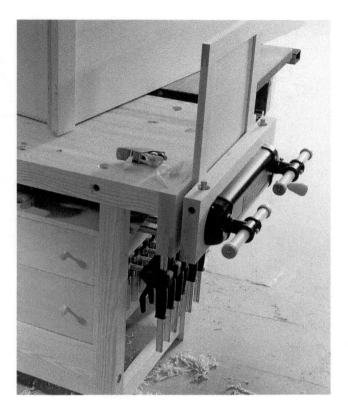

Tail vise. A tail vise is a luxury we all deserve. Since adding one to my bench at home, shown here, I've found myself using it far more than a face vise.

shoot your work across the room, easily puncturing any foam cooler in its path. Don't ask me how I know this.

The most versatile planing stop is a piece of ½"-thick plywood that is as long as your bench is wide. A couple wing nuts, bolts, and washers (see top right photo, p. 154) allow you to position and fix the stop up and down, depending on the thickness of your workpiece.

The hardware is readily available at any home center. The part that is driven into the bench is sold as a ¼" x 20 screw-in insert nut. To install it, first drill a ⅜"-diameter hole in the end of your bench. Coat the hole with epoxy and drive the insert in slowly using a (usually metric) hex wrench. Then, thread a 1¼"-long bolt through a ¼" x 20 wing nut and a ¼"-hole washer.

Planing stop (left). If you use a hand plane, you really should invest the small amount of money and an hour of your time to make this planing stop. It is the most versatile stop I've ever used and works for thick or thin stock.

Proper hardware (right). The key to the planing stop is the hardware. Here you can see how the ¼" x 20 screw-in insert nut, 1 ¼"-long bolt, ¼" x 20 wing nut, and ¼"-hole washer are assembled.

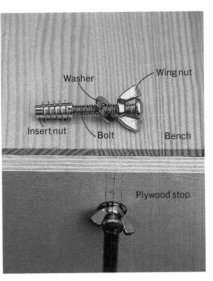

The stop itself is plywood with two stopped slots that measure ⁵⁄₁₆"-wide. Make the slots long enough so your stop can go below the edge of your bench.

This stop allows you to plane wood of almost any thickness. Unscrew the wing nuts, adjust the stop where you want it, and tighten the wing nuts to hold the stop in place.

7. ADD A HOLDFAST

Sometimes you need to hold a board on your bench so you can work on its end, such as when you're chiseling out the waste between dovetails. Nothing is as quick or efficient at this job as a quality holdfast.

A holdfast is essentially a hook that drops into a hole in your bench. You tighten it with a screw or rap it with a mallet to lock the work to your bench.

There are three major types that are worth purchasing. The most expensive drops easily into any ¾" hole in your bench and is tightened by turning a screw on the top. I've used

this type of holdfast every day for years and it has never let me down.

The second option is more economical. Glass-filled nylon hold-down clamps are cheap, but you have to reach under your benchtop to operate them.

The third type is a metal hook. Rap the top to tighten it and rap the back to release it. All of the versions I've seen in catalogs are cast metal and don't work well for me. My fellow hand-tool enthusiasts recommend forged holdfasts, which are hand-made by blacksmiths. It's worth asking around in your area if there's a blacksmith who will do this work for you.

8. ADD A SHARPENING AND FINISHING TRAY

While some people might accuse me of just being fastidious, there are sound reasons to protect your bench from sharpening slurry and finishing materials.

Sharpening slurry is made up of bits of metal and abrasive that will dig into your bench and later get embedded in your work. And finishing materials (dyes, stains, and glazes in particular) can rub off on your work for weeks or years if they spill on your bench.

That's why a tray with a low lip is ideal for typical sharpening and finishing jobs. I make my trays from inexpensive plywood with a lip made of ¾"-thick scrap pieces—plus glue and screws. The best thing about the tray is that it drops into two dog holes, so there's no need to clamp it in place. This makes the tray especially good for sharpening because the tray stays put as you work.

9. A TOP JUST FOR GLUING

Not all of us have the luxury of a separate bench for assembly, so I end up constructing most of my furniture right on my bench—both at work and at home.

Getting glue on the bench is a big problem most woodworkers face. Yellow glue, which is mostly water, isn't good for your top because you're introducing moisture in places where it has spilled. And dried glue can easily mar your work.

So, I have a removable top that fits right over my benchtop for gluing chores. It's made using ⅛"-thick hardboard (available at your local home center store) and four cleats that keep it securely in place on the benchtop.

Why not use newspaper or a blanket? Well, newspaper makes a lot of waste, and is slow and messy. Blankets, if not perfectly flat on your bench, can actually introduce a little twist in your glue-ups. If you don't want to make a hardboard glue-up

CUT LIST & MATERIALS						
	NO.	ITEM	DIMENSIONS (INCHES)			MATERIAL
			T	W	L	
PLANING AND SANDING STOP						
☐	1	Screw-in insert nut	¼–20			
☐	1	Bolt			1 ¼	
☐	1	Wing nut	¼–20			
☐	1	Washer	¼			
☐	1	Stop	½		*	Plywood
VISE BLOCKS						
☐	1	Block	½	½	†	Pine
☐	1	Block	⅝	⅝	†	Pine
☐	1	Block	¾	¾	†	Pine
☐	1	Block	⅞	⅞	†	Pine
☐	1	Block	1	1	†	Pine
☐	6	Hanging pegs	¾–dia.		3	Dowel

* Match the width of your bench. † Match the depth of your vise jaws.

top, the next-best option is to buy a thin plastic tablecloth.

10. VISE BLOCKS ADD BITE

One of the biggest complaints woodworkers have with their vise is that it doesn't hold the work very well when they clamp using only one side of the jaw. The jaw bends a little bit—especially with wooden vises—and this weakens its grip on the work.

The solution is so simple I'm surprised that I don't see this more often. Put a block of equal thickness on the other side of the jaw and your problem is solved. I have a set of "vise blocks" in the most common thicknesses I deal with (½", ⅝", ¾", ⅞" and 1"). To help me out even more, I drive a ¾" dowel through each block to prevent it from dropping when I release the vise. This quick and simple fix will save you a lot of future frustration. ■

SLIDING DEADMAN PLANS

As mentioned in item 2, "A Deadman Lends a Hand" (p. 150), there are few clamping jobs that are more difficult than trying to secure something big so that you can work on its edge. Mor–tising a large door for a hinge is a common situation. Cleaning up the long edge of a board you just bandsawed is another.

These problems are quickly and easily solved by taking a lesson from 18th-century joiners. A common feature on older benches is what's called a "sliding deadman." This contraption works with your face vise to support work that is long, wide, or both. I adapted mine from a sketch by Graham Blackburn that was featured in his excellent book *Traditional Woodworking Handtools* (photo on p. 148). You should customize the sizes of the rails and the sliding deadman to fit your bench.

After you determine the proper dimensions for all your parts, begin by cutting your pieces to rough size. Cut a ⅜"-deep x 9/16"-wide groove in the center of a long edge of each rail. Use a dado stack in your table saw, a straight bit in your router, or a plough plane to cut the groove.

Before you cut the curves on the deadman itself, bore the ⅝"-diameter holes through the part for the ledge. I bored two staggered rows of holes; each hole is 2" down from the one above it. The topmost hole is located so that when the ledge is in place in the deadman, it lines up with the rails on my face vise.

Cut the ½"-long x ½"-thick tenons on both ends of the deadman. The tenons are slightly thinner than the width of the grooves they ride in. Cut the deadman to shape. The long edges are curved in ⅞" so they are easy to grasp when the deadman is resting against your bench's legs. Round over the long edges of the deadman to make it friendly to grasp. I used a ¼" roundover bit in a router.

Trim your rails to the proper length; install them. Screw one rail to the bottom rail of your bench using four #8 x 2" screws. Don't use glue; you want to be able to remove the rail for later adjustments or repairs. Put the top rail and deadman in place and line them up with the bottom rail. Using screws, secure the top rail to the underside of your bench's top, or to the top rail of your bench—if you have one. Wax the grooves in the rails. The deadman should slide back and forth with minimal effort.

Now, make the ledge. You could simply use a dowel. I chose to make one a little fancier. Bore a 1¼"-deep hole in one end for the ⅝" dowel and glue it in place, again making sure that when the ledge is inserted into the top hole, it lines up with the rails on your face vise. You might need to sand your dowel to fit the holes in the deadman. I used a ¼" beading bit in a router to shape three edges of each side of the ledge. Finish your deadman to match your bench.

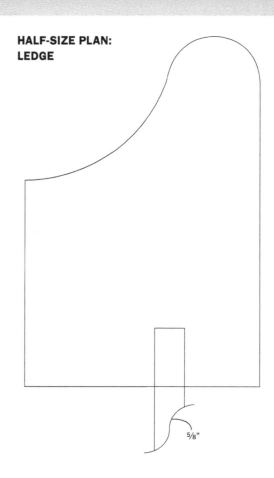

HALF-SIZE PLAN: LEDGE

⅝"

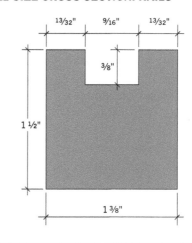

FULL-SIZE CROSS SECTION: RAILS

13/32"   9/16"   13/32"

⅜"

1 ½"

1 ⅜"

FRONT VIEW

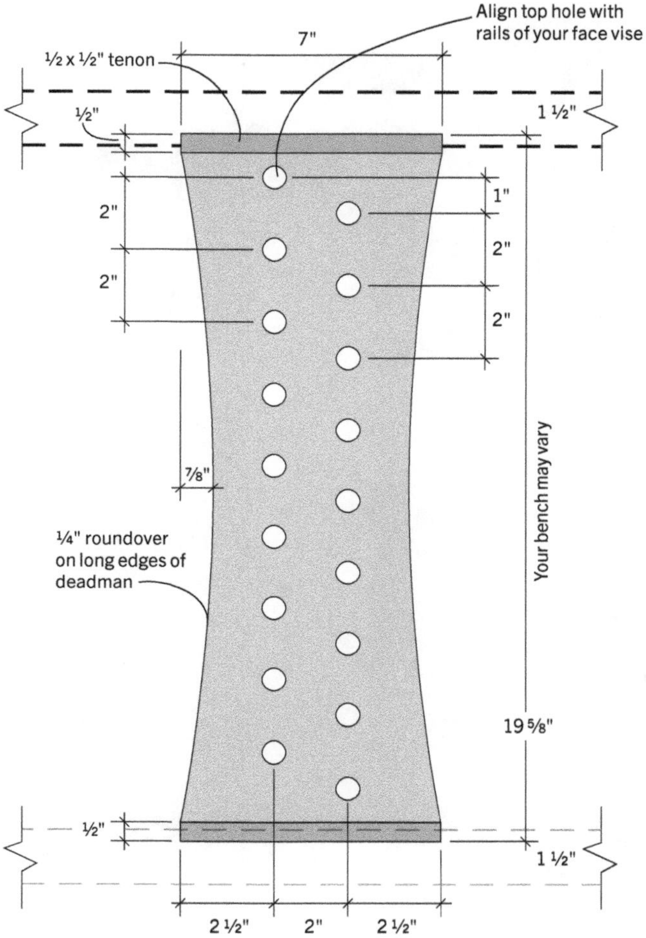

CROSS SECTION

Align top hole with
rails of your face vise

7"

½ x ½" tenon

½"

1 ½"

2"

2"

1"

2"

2"

⅞"

Your bench may vary

¼" roundover
on long edges of
deadman

19 ⅝"

½"

1 ½"

2 ½"   2"   2 ½"

1 ⅜"

Secure top
rail to bottom
of benchtop
or top rail of
bench

Secure bottom
rail to bottom
rail of bench

CUT LIST & MATERIALS

	NO.	ITEM	DIMENSIONS (INCHES)			MATERIAL	COMMENTS
			T	W	L		
☐	2	Rails	1 ⅜	1 ½	47*	SYP†	
☐	1	Deadman	1 ⅜	7	19 ⅝‡	SYP	½" TBE§
☐	1	Ledge	1 ⅜	4 ⅞	7 ½	SYP	
☐	1	Dowel	⅝-dia.		5		

* Match the length of your bench. † SYP= Southern yellow pine or equivalent. ‡ Match
the height of your workbench. § TBE = Tenon both ends.

HOLD EVERYTHING
(WITH ALMOST NOTHING)

You can hold anything on your workbench with just pegs, wedges, and notches—no fancy vises required.

BY CHRISTOPHER SCHWARZ

t's difficult for most woodworkers to imagine a workbench without screw-driven vises. But for most of human history, that's how it worked. No matter what you were building—furniture, wagons, barrels, or houses—the workbench was typically a strong table with a collection of pegs, wedges, and notches.

While screw-driven vises have existed since Roman times, they didn't show up on workbenches until about the 14th century. And even in the 18th century, many woodworkers still preferred simple benches without screw-driven vises.

For today's woodworker, I think there are many reasons to understand and consider alternatives to the modern workbench. For one, they let you transform almost any surface into a workbench—even a picnic table. So, you don't have to leave your shop behind while on vacation.

They also are a great way to get a fully functional bench without spending much money. All of these contrivances use scraps—plus maybe a holdfast or clamp. You don't

The lockjaw stop. This French bench uses rusty nails to secure the work. I have yet to cut myself on a metal planing stop during the last 12 years. So, this looks worse than it really is.

Wide planing stop. Add a thin batten in front of your planing stop, and you've made an effective planing stop for wide panels.

have to spend thousands on a bench to build your first birdhouse.

Finally, these workholding methods are just as effective as modern vises. In some cases, they are actually superior. Let's begin with my favorite—the single-point planing stop.

THE PLANING STOP
On early workbenches, the planing stop was the foundation for all the other bits of workholding. In fact,

It's in the hip. This is how I typically deal with wide stock. Keep the plane in line with the planing stop (left). Shift the board toward you as you work (center). When you reach the far edge, use your hip to press the board against the stop (right). If you have a face vise, move its jaw out to help support the board as well.

A kick to your backside. With the doe's foot behind the work you can plane wide panels parallel to the grain or across it.

some benches are equipped with only a planing stop.

Most planing stops are comprised of a square stick that's long enough to penetrate the benchtop and give you enough height for planing boards on edge—3" x 3" x 12" is typical. The stop is adjusted up and down with mallet blows, so it needs to be a durable, dry wood.

You might think that fitting the planing stop requires you to consider how wet the benchtop is and the current season. Will the stop and benchtop (or both) shrink as they dry? There are formulas and lots speculation for how tight or loose to make things. Ignore them.

When I fit a planing stop, I assume that I'm going to have to adjust it later on if it becomes too tight or make a new one if things get too loose. So, I focus on getting a good snug fit that day. I want the stop to move about ⅛" with each heavy mallet blow.

After I get that fit, I simply pay attention to how it functions. If the stop becomes almost impossible to move, I remove it and plane it a tad. If it's too loose, you can glue some veneer onto the existing stop or make a new one. In time, the wood will settle down and your planing stop will do the same.

Most planing stops have some toothed metal on their tops to help secure the work. This can be as simple as a few nails driven through the stop. Other woodworkers attach a bit of saw steel to the top of the planing stop and file teeth into it. Still others use a blacksmith-made stop or a commercial version.

They all work. File the teeth sharp and your work will move a lot less. And before you start planing a board, give the board a whack on its far end with a mallet so the teeth bite hard into the end grain of your work.

If you want to avoid getting teeth marks in a particular piece of wood, muzzle the teeth with a stick of wood. I use a stick of wood that is as long as my benchtop is wide. One end goes against the teeth. The other end is secured with a holdfast. It's an instant wide planing stop.

The wide planing stop is a crutch, and sometimes you really need it. But I suggest you try to plane wide boards with the stop alone and see what you can get away with. By slightly shifting the work, you can control fairly wide boards. With practice, 8"-wide boards are no problem. Then shoot for 12".

DOE'S FOOT

Once you install a planing stop, the first accessory you should make for it is a "doe's foot," a simple appliance that plays nice with the planing stop. Instructions for making your

Every little bit helps. This shallow mortise in the underside of the palm helps prevent the palm from coming loose from the planing stop.

The palm. This versatile planing stop can be used for dressing faces or edges of boards.

own are on page 172. The doe's foot is simply a piece of wood of almost any size with a 90° notch cut into its end. The device works by allowing your workpiece to get snagged in the notch between the two "toes" of the foot, immobilizing it from behind.

THE MOVABLE PALM

When a doe's foot is used in front of the work instead of behind it, it's sometimes called a "palm." The word comes from the Chinese legend of how planing stops were invented. (Hint: It involved making a device instead of using a person's palm to secure the work.)

Palms show up on many early workbenches and are an extra-fancy version of a planing stop. I made one that can be moved up and down like a planing stop, and it works great.

It's about ½" x 7" x 13" with a V cut into one end. I attached the palm to the top of a 2" x 2" x 8" planing stop with glue and nails.

Because the palm is thin, I took pains to attach it to the planing stop so it wouldn't be wrenched off—planing stops take heaps of abuse. So, this palm is attached via a shallow mortise, glue, and two beefy Roman-style nails.

Chop a ¼"-deep mortise in the underside of your palm to receive the end of the planing stop. Use a router plane to ensure the bottom of the mortise is flat so the palm and planing stop will join at right angles.

Roman nails hold like the dickens but will split the work if you are careless in drilling pilot holes and clearance holes. While the palm is disassembled, drill clearance holes in the mortise for two beefy nails.

Glue the planing stop into the mortise, checking to ensure the stop is perpendicular to the palm all around. Once the glue is dry, drill pilot holes into the end of the planing stop. The depth of the holes should be equal to about two-thirds the length of your

Don't monkey around. Here is a reproduction of the painting of Karl Schreyner made by my daughter, Katy Schwarz. Note that Schreyner wasn't a monkey—Katy just drew him that way.

nail (about 1 ½" deep in my case) and slightly smaller than the shaft of the nail. Nail the palm to the planing stop and you are done.

SIDE STOPS: SCHREYNER PEGS

In addition to the doe's foot and palm, there are other ways to prevent the work from spinning to the side while you plane it. One of the simplest is a method shown in a painting circa 1425 of woodworker Karl Schreyner at his bench.

The painting shows two round pegs at the end of the bench that work like simple planing stops. There are two additional pegs that restrain a board from the side. This painting is part of a series of over 1,000 famous paintings of Nuremberg craftsmen

now called "The Mendel and Landauer Hausbücher," and are a rich source of information on early crafts.

While many craftsmen are shown in the Mendel and Landauer paintings working at their benches, the painting of Schreyner is the only one I'm aware of where the workbench has these pegs to the side of the work. And so I plan to call these "Schreyner pegs" until I find an earlier source (or a catchier name).

Here's how I installed the Schreyner pegs on my benchtop. I started with a 1"-diameter x 36"-long oak dowel. Then, I sawed it into seven 5"-long bits. I then laid out the positions of the 1" holes. The end stops are located where a simple planing stop would usually go. One is 4 ½" from the front edge of the bench. The second is 11" from the front edge.

The pegs for the side are all 13 ½" from the front edge of the bench. The first peg is 3" to the right of the end stops. The remainder are positioned on 12" centers.

LAYOUT: SCHREYNER PEGS

Across the board. For short boards, you'll need to shift the work left or right occasionally to keep the board under control. This is not a big deal.

With the board. Planing boards 6" to 10" wide can be a little tricky because the work is restrained by only one end stop and can rotate. You can fix this by putting a batten in front of the two end stops, making a wide planing stop.

Drive the 1" pegs into the holes. They should require mallet taps to move up or down. Now, you have a system of pegs that can handle traversing or planing with the grain.

ROMAN SIDE STOPS

Similar to the Schreyner pegs are the side stops found on the earliest surviving workbench (circa 187 AD) at the Roman fort in Saalburg, Germany. Like pegs, these stops move up and down and restrain the edges of boards and work in conjunction with the planing stop.

I first found these Saalburg side stops on a Roman bench that was both low and narrow, but they can be installed on workbenches of any height (they show up in historical paintings on taller benches). Like the Schreyner pegs, they can be used on their own for traversing boards with a handplane. Or, they can be used in conjunction with a planing stop to prevent wide boards from spinning while planing them.

They also can be used like a bench hook for sawing joinery. Press the work against the side stops and cut tenon shoulders or dado walls.

OTHER WAYS TO USE PEGS

Many early benches, especially knee-high ones, feature a series of peg holes that form a long and shallow V-shape down the middle of the benchtop's length. I've been working with this system of holes and pegs for a couple years and have found it surprisingly versatile.

The pegs for these holes can be as much as 6" tall, which allows them to support work when you work on the edge of a board. Here's how: Put one peg at the bottom of the V. Place your board on edge against that peg. Now look down the two legs of the V for two holes—one on each face of the board—and put pegs in those holes. These pegs support your work from both sides. Now, you'll find it remarkably easy to edge plane boards.

I've got this pegged. By having a selection of pegs that vary in length and girth, you'll find it easy to secure most boards on the benchtop.

LAYOUT: ROMAN BENCH PEG

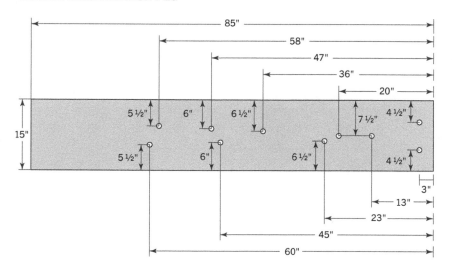

Be seated. When traversing boards on a low bench, sit on a sawbench (or any low seat) to get the job done. Yes, it's OK to sit when you work.

Bench stops. Traversing short boards is simple; with longer stock, I use a stool or sawbench to support the end hanging off the benchtop.

For working on the faces of boards, many of these benches had two movable pegs at the end of the bench that could be used much like the Schreyner pegs mentioned earlier. While many of the operations are the same as with the Schreyner pegs, you also use your body to restrain the work when you plane long boards.

Once you get into boards that are longer than your arms can reach, you sit on the work. With workpieces longer than 40", I begin by processing the stock close to the planing stops as shown above. When that section is planed, I scoot backward about 3' and repeat the process.

Traversing boards with a fore plane is also fairly easy with the low bench. You brace the work against the planing stops, then use your knees to lock everything tight

against the stops. Finally, plane the area between your legs. An outboard sawbench helps support long stock or when you are at the beginning or end of a particular board.

You can also use the pegs at the end to secure your work similarly when sawing dados or chiseling waste across the grain.

NOTCHES AND WEDGES

In many old woodworking paintings, you'll see benches that have no vises but instead have a large rectangular notch cut into the edge or end of the benchtop. In many cases, these notches are used as face vises. You put the work in the notch and then use a wedge to immobilize it. I've had great—actually, quite spectacular—success using these notches for cutting tenons and shaping the work with chisels, rasps, and files.

It took a little experimentation, however, to get the wedges right. In the end, I went to my scrap pile and grabbed a white pine 2x4. I sawed it to 12" long and tapered one edge with a jack plane (I later measured the angle at 2°). Then I drove it into a notch.

It cinched down as hard as any screw-driven vise I've used. It worked so well that I laughed out loud.

If you are interested in making these notches, here are some details. On some benches, the notches are in the end of the benchtop. In others, they are cut into the edges. I tried both. They both held just fine.

Making the two kinds of notches, however, is quite different. The end grain notches take twice as long to make because the wood is fighting you the entire time. You have to rip saw the walls of the notch and then

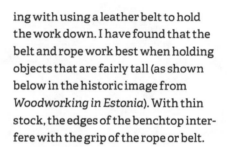

Quick work. With the notch on the edge, you saw the walls and pry the waste out easily with a chisel. Then, clean the long grain of the notch with paring cuts.

Tap that. Knock the softwood wedge between the work and the benchtop (left) and the work is secure enough for any operation (right).

chisel out the waste like cutting a huge dovetail. There is a lot of chopping and splitting. It's not a horrible task, but it's more difficult than creating a notch in the edge of the benchtop.

There you crosscut the walls (crosscutting is easier than ripping). Split the waste with chisel chops. Splitting wood along the grain is always easier than chopping across it.

Here are the measurements for my notches. Don't feel compelled to copy me, however. The end-grain notch is 4 ½" wide and 2 ½" long. The edge notch is 4 ¼" long and 2" wide. I have a variety of softwood wedges scattered about that can handle work from 1" wide to 3" wide.

BELTS AND ROPES
One bonus operation: You can hold assemblies to the benchtop to work on their faces using a rope (or a belt) and your feet to create a primitive vise. I first saw this in an Egyptian painting. I've also been experiment-

ing with using a leather belt to hold the work down. I have found that the belt and rope work best when holding objects that are fairly tall (as shown below in the historic image from *Woodworking in Estonia*). With thin stock, the edges of the benchtop interfere with the grip of the rope or belt.

Gag order. A rope makes a surprisingly good hold-down, as seen in this old photograph, where a cooper has made a simple slab-style bench into an effective shavehorse (from *Woodworking in Estonia*).

Workbenches don't have to be fancy to do their job gracefully. Our ancestors could build masterpieces with simpler tools and workbenches, and so can we. It just takes a little imagination and an open mind. ■

SHOP-MADE TAIL VISE

Transform your workbench with custom-fit workholding.

BY CHRISTOPHER SCHWARZ

For many woodworkers, especially those of the Galoot persuasion, a workbench with a tail vise of some sort is a fundamental necessity. These vises are integral to most European-style benches, and there are now extraordinary after-market options. But what are your choices if you don't happen to possess one, or if one of the manufactured vises doesn't fit your needs? Many off-the-shelf options require either extreme modifications to an existing workbench, or the construction of a new bench altogether.

One of the great benefits of craft skills, for me, is the ability to change and form my immediate working environment to fit my preferences and expand my productive capacity. The recent addition of a shop-made tail vise to my old torsion-box workbench demonstrates this perfectly. You can easily adopt and adapt the principles and construction techniques I used to your own situation.

The resulting accessory is sophisticated and elegant, and it transforms your bench. But it does not require extraordinary tools or equipment to make. If you have access to a good table saw, drill press, and a few standard hand tools, and have reasonable measuring and layout skills, you can knock this out in less than a day.

My bench has a torsion-box top rather than a solid slab, so most of the available products were not viable. Instead, using parts mostly from industrial supply vendors and some ½" Baltic birch plywood, I was able to retrofit my bench with an excellent tail vise. It nestled exactly into the space I had to perfectly serve my needs.

This "add-on" feature employs the long-standing concept basic to all tail vises—a fixed dog embedded into the top of the bench paired with a in-line moving dog—to provide the holding function for my workpiece. The end result is a bolt-on enhancement that can immediately change both your work habits and capacity.

I had two design considerations. The first was the unalterable dimensions involved. My benchtop is 5" thick, and the length of the space available for a retrofit along the front edge of the bench was 32". Sec-

Quad-layer spacers. Blocks of four layers of Baltic birch plywood are glued with hot hide glue and standard shop clamps. All of the wood components in this project are Baltic birch plywood.

EXPLODED VIEW

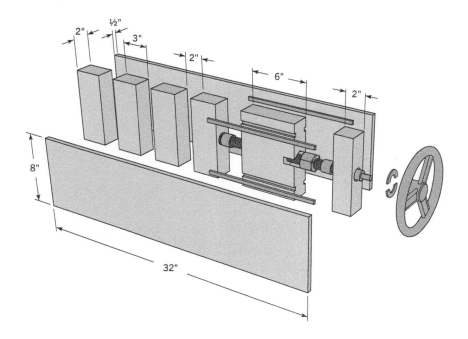

Exacting setup. This cross-feed table on my drill press facilitates drilling the concentric holes for the screw and bronze sleeve bushings. Start with the larger hole first, then the smaller hole inside.

ond was my increasing attraction to wheel-handled vises. I decided to give my vise an 8"-diameter recycled wheel handle, which required me to design the vise so the wheel did not extend above the benchtop.

Construction began by cutting the 8" x 32" front and rear plates, and gluing up some quadruple-laminated spacer blocks made from Baltic birch plywood. The blocks are the same width as the plates.

The size of these pieces reflected both the bench thickness and the depth necessary for the hand wheel to fit on the screw that drove the moving carriage back and forth. One of the blocks is used at the business end of the unit as the platform for laying out and assembling the guts of the vise. A second block fits near the mid-point of the unit, as I later describe.

CUT LIST & MATERIALS

	NO.	ITEM	DIMENSIONS (INCHES)			MATERIAL
			T	W	L	
☐	2	Front/rear plates	½	8	32	Baltic birch plywood
☐	1	Wheel end block	2	2	8	Baltic birch plywood
☐	1	Carriage block	2	6	8	Baltic birch plywood
☐	4	Spacer blocks	2	3	8	Baltic birch plywood
☐	1	Left-hand Acme thread stock*	1-dia.			
☐	4	Left-hand Acme nuts*	1-dia.			
☐	1	Wheel		8-dia.		Cast iron
☐	2	Washers, 1 3/16 ID				Stainless steel
☐	1	Ways	3/8	¼	36	Steel bar stock
☐		Bushings	1	1 ¼	1	Bronze sleeve

* 4 threads per inch.

BUILD THE CARRIAGE

The next step is to decide the length of the movable-dog carriage, and how much you want it to move. These are essentially arbitrary choices. I chose a 6"-long carriage with 6" of travel. On the other hand, these are not entirely whimsical decisions because they determine the spacing of the fixed dog holes. In other words, if your carriage travels 4", you need to have fixed dog holes every 4" down the length of the vise. After this was established, I cut the 2"-thick blocks to serve as my dog spacers, and my carriage.

The dimensions of the end blocks were determined after the rest of the structure was laid out and assembled. Prior to constructing the moving carriage block, glue the spacer blocks to either the front or rear plate.

In this tail-vise configuration, the carriage moves along a threaded rod that penetrates horizontally through it. The rod also runs through a nut attached to the carriage. I chose left-handed, or reverse thread, 1" Acme-thread stock because it makes the carriage work similar to a typical end vise.

To install the setup, I first established the top-to-bottom centerline of the wheel handle, and the front-to-back centerline of the carriage block on both ends. I then drilled a hole in one end to accommodate a bronze sleeve bearing for the trailing end of the threaded rod. On the other end I drilled a 1" hole to fit the threaded rod itself.

Because my drill press does not have enough travel to do the job in one step, I drilled the hole as deep as the press would allow, then retracted

Quickly defined. A simple backsaw makes it quite easy to cut the outlines for the cavity into which the nut will go.

Sitting just right. Fitting the nut is perhaps the fussiest part of the whole project. Make sure it aligns with the thread-screw hole and is flush with the surface.

the bit. I raised the drill press table to where the drill bit fit inside the workpiece hole, clamped everything in place, and finished the hole through to the opposite side.

I don't own—and hope to never have to purchase—any left-hand thread taps and dies. I needed to install the left-hand thread, 1" Acme nut into the carriage block to serve as the engagement for the threaded rod. I threaded the nut onto the rod, inserted it into the carriage block, then marked the outline of the nut on the block.

Using a backsaw, I sawed the lines of this hexagonal outline, then excavated the cavity with a hammer and chisels until the nut seated firmly and squarely in the void. I then attached the nut to the carriage with screws through countersunk holes drilled through the nut.

THE CARRIAGE GUIDES

The last phase for the carriage was to create guides or "ways" that keep the

One at each turn. I drilled and countersunk six holes around the perimeter of the nut, then screwed it into the carriage block's hexagonal cavity.

carriage riding square while in use. (Almost any hard, smooth material will suffice for the ways, but I chose steel stock from my scrap drawer.)

With a dado stack, I cut ⅜" x ¼" grooves about 1" from the top and bottom edges of the carriage, on both the front and back plates. I drilled three small countersink holes into each of the four rectangular rods to allow easy attachment to the inner faces of the front and rear plates.

Locating the ways is easy. Place the carriage against the inside of

the rear plate in the correct position, making sure to get the block aligned exactly with the top of the plate. Insert two of the ways into the carriage block with the countersunk side up, then attach the ways to the plate with appropriate-sized flathead screws. Repeat on the other plate.

Your choice for dogs in the moving carriage is entirely up to you. Removable doweled blocks work fine as a dog on the top of the carriage, as do rising bench stops or a simple threaded set screw.

At some point I'll try to talk myself into installing fancy dovetailed dogs (like those on H. O. Studley's bench) into each end of the carriage, but for now any of the former options work fine, as will a large screw countersunk to be level with the top surface of the carriage.

FINAL ASSEMBLY

Once the carriage was completed, I drilled a hole in the first fixed spacer block to accommodate another bronze sleeve bearing, and glued the

Just like this. Here, you can see the complete moving carriage setup prior to final assembly.

Two methods. I elected to use removable dowel blocks and a simple threaded set screw for my moving carriage.

block in place—this bearing assures a wobble-free performance for the carriage until long after my ashes are spread on the mountain behind my barn. The remaining spacer blocks were glued in place based on the dimensions of the dogs themselves. I chose square cross-section dogs that measure 2"x 2", and are 8" long.

On the back of the fixed block at the wheel end of the setup, I drilled a precise hole to hold a final sleeve bearing.

On the handled end of the threaded screw, I had to grind, file, or machine the rod to accommodate the wheel. Then, I dry-fit the assembly, including the movable carriage, its two retaining blocks, and the hand wheel.

With the pieces all in position, I noted the outer surface of the fixed-end block on the rod. This locates where to cut a groove around the circumference of the thread stock for a garter.

The fittings to retain the drive screw are standard ¾" inside-diameter washers—to make the connection robust, I used two washers stacked together.

The outside measurement for the drive screw is 1", so I figured an ⅛"-deep groove the width of two washers would be easy enough to cut with a file (or with my machine lathe, if it came to that).

I marked and drilled the screw holes on my drill press, although a handheld drill would certainly suffice.

After drilling the holes with both washers aligned, I countersunk the holes on the outer washer. Using a hacksaw, I cut each washer in two,

with the cutline turned 90° from the outer washer to the inner washer. This ensured unbreakable strength for the composite garter.

The only thing left is to assemble the entire unit, attach it to your bench, and get to work. I found my vise to be a bit stiff at first as all the pieces were seating in, but once that happened, it worked smoothly and easily.

By following and adapting the ideas here, I believe you too can add a moving-dog tail vise to your workbench. The advantages are to make your bench exactly the way you want, and to avoid making a new bench or radically modify an existing bench. Plus, it provides the undeniable pleasure of making something exceedingly useful. It just might change forever the character and capability of your bench and the way you approach our craft. ◼

Get the job done. While a lathe makes this step effortless, careful use of a grinding wheel and file can accomplish the same end, although not quite as beautifully.

Ingenuity at work. The split garter is actually a pair of split washers in disguise. The end of the rod is modified to accept the hand wheel.

DOE'S FOOT

These notched sticks simplify your workholding at the bench.

BY CHRISTOPHER SCHWARZ

I first became fascinated by the doe's foot after seeing U.K. woodworker Richard Maguire use one in lieu of a tail vise. And after several years of research and trials at my own bench, the doe's foot has become an indispensable part of my workholding.

It's a fiendishly clever and simple appliance. Even if you have a work-bench with all the bells and whistles, you'll find a doe's foot useful in a pinch. Plus, if you ever work on-site without a workbench—or on a picnic table on vacation—the doe's foot is a lifesaver.

HOW DOES IT WORK?
The doe's foot is simply a piece of wood of almost any size with a 90°

notch cut into its end. The device works by allowing your workpiece to get snagged in the notch between the two "toes" of the foot, immobilizing it.

The doe's foot can be used both in front of the work or behind. It can be secured to the benchtop with a holdfast, clamps, pegs, or even nails driven through the doe's foot and into the benchtop.

To get started, I recommend you make one that is ½" x 7" x 12". Cut a 90° notch at one end (as shown) that leaves a ¼" flat at the corners. We'll call these flats the "toes."

You may need to apply adhesive-backed sandpaper, rubber treads for ladder rungs, or cork to if the doe foot slips in use.

IN FRONT OF THE WORK

In some old paintings, you'll see the doe's foot used in front of the work instead of a planing stop. In many ways, I have found the doe's foot to be more useful than the traditional single-point planing stop. Here's why.

A single-point stop is great for planing narrow stock; pretty much anything less than 6" wide is easy to control against the stop. But once you start planing wider stock, things get tricky. You either have to keep moving the stock or skew the plane just right to prevent the wood from spinning on the benchtop.

With a doe's foot, you plane narrow stock by pressing it between the toes. With wider stock, you press it against the two toes, forcing the doe's foot to act as a wide planing stop.

Note that this works when planing boards on their faces or on their edges. The doe's foot is quite effective

for planing narrow boards on their edges.

But what about planing even wider panels, such as an 18"-wide side of a typical chest of drawers? That's when you move the doe's foot so it's behind the work.

BEHIND THE WORK

Some people don't believe this technique works until they try it. So if you are doubtful, give it a whirl before you dismiss it.

For planing wide panels, push the front of your workpiece against a planing stop (or a doe's foot). Then place the notch of a doe's foot against the far corner of the rear of the board. (Look at the photo on p. 172—it's simpler than my words suggest.) Secure the doe's foot against the benchtop—I use a holdfast.

Now, you can plane the board either with the grain or across the grain. Yup, the doe's foot is a lifesaver for traversing. Planing across the grain wedges your board against both the planing stop and the doe's foot like magic.

For me, that was the moment I knew I didn't need a tail vise. Armed with a couple of doe's feet and a pair of holdfasts, there's almost nothing I cannot do to a piece of wood when building furniture. ■

CUT LIST & MATERIALS

	NO.	ITEM	DIMENSIONS (INCHES)			MATERIAL
			T	W	L	
☐	1	Doe's foot	½	7	12	Hardwood

Best foot forward. With the doe's foot in front of the work, it can wedge narrow pieces (top) or support wider work with its tippy-toes (bottom).

MAKE A RAAMTANG

This Dutch joiner's tool leverages simple design into a cheap and effective workholding device.

BY ZACHARY DILLINGER

While studying Gerrit van der Sterre's *Four Centuries of Dutch Planes and Planemakers*, I ran across what the author calls a "raamtang"—Dutch for "window pliers." As you might guess, it is a joiner's tool used originally to hold narrow window sash bars for molding.

The similarities between this entirely shop-made wedge-powered vise and the screw-powered Moxon vise led me to make and try a raamtang with great success for other work.

HEART OF OAK

There is a lot of force exerted on the jaws of a raamtang—so much that they often bend in use. To counteract this, I chose to make mine from strong white oak.

The version of the raamtang presented here is long enough to hold up to a 24"-wide panel and stock up to about 1½" thick. Feel free to make modifications to suit the scale of work you do in your shop, but this size works well for most furniture tasks.

Prepare your ¾"-thick wedge blank and mark out the angle, then saw the pieces apart and plane the sawn edge to a smooth surface.

I like to use about a 15° or 20° angle, but the exact angle of the wedge is unimportant because you will lay out the shoulder cut from the wedge. Just remember—a shallow angle will hold with more strength than a steep angle.

STRONG ARM TACTICS

Use straight-grained white oak for the arms. For the jaws, pick up some 6/4 white oak a little more than 4" wide.

Rough-plane both faces and pick the most attractive grain pattern to serve as the top side of the vise. After that, flatten that face with your try plane. This will serve as the reference face, so make sure it is as flat as you can make it.

Next, set a marking gauge to the thinnest dimension present between the two faces of the board and mark a line all the way around. Plane the board down to this thickness, but save the final smoothing until after you've chopped the mortises.

Joint the first edge of your board. When finished, this will serve as your reference edge for laying out the arm mortises. Mark out and plane the width of the board so that it is about 4" wide, then scribe a line on each face that is 2" from the reference edge.

Because you want the mortises in both arms to line up, lay them both out at the same time before separating the jaws with your rip saw.

Start by establishing the inside lines of the mortises so that they are 24" apart. Align the arms with those lines and mark out their width along the top face. Square these four lines down both edges using the top face for the stock of the square.

OPEN THE JAWS

Now saw the jaws apart with your ripsaw. Place the separated jaws on your benchtop with the reference edge down, then square the sawn edges with your try plane, planing a slight crown on the inside edge of the rear jaw.

Memory help. Plane the wedges to a consistent angle. This frees you from having to remember which wedge goes to which arm.

Square deal. Keep the stock of the square tight against your blanks while keeping the arm blank tight against the blade of the square.

A tight grip. The slight crown in the rear jaw will provide maximum holding power near the center of the vise.

Lignin biceps. Here are the raamtang arms in their final shape.

Strike zone. I prefer to strike my mortise layout lines with a sharp bench chisel.

Smooth action. This arm has a nice loose fit through the rear jaw; this will enable the vise to work without binding.

EXPLODED VIEW

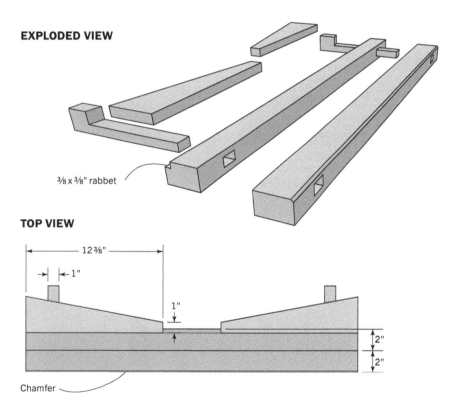

3⁄8 x 3⁄8" rabbet

TOP VIEW

12 3⁄8"

1"

1"

2"

2"

Chamfer

Square mortise lines down the sawn edges from the reference face. Finally, lay out a 3⁄8" x 3⁄8" rabbet along the top back edge of the rear jaw; this engages with the wedges and helps them stay aligned when you drive them into place.

Lay out and saw the angled cuts on the top of the arms using the wedges as templates. Next, scribe the 5⁄8" tongue, referencing the face of the marking gauge off what will be the bottom face of the arms. Rip the waste material away close to the line, then smooth the rough-sawn face of the tongue down to your line with planes and chisels.

Save the sawed-off waste to make the pegs that attach the arms to the front jaw. Finally, drill a pilot hole, then drive a rosehead nail into the center of the remaining thick portion to help prevent shearing this piece off in use.

CHOP THE ARM MORTISES

Set a marking gauge to the thickness of the arm tongues so the fence is 3⁄8" away from the first tooth. Scribe the mortises on both edges down from

CUT LIST & MATERIALS

	NO.	ITEM	DIMENSIONS (INCHES)			MATERIAL	COMMENTS
			T	W	L		
☐	2	Jaws	1 3⁄8	2	30	White oak	
☐	2	Arms	1 1⁄2	1	8	White oak	
☐	2	Wedges	3⁄4	3 3⁄8	12 3⁄8	White oak	Taper to 1"

the top of the jaws. If you have a mortise chisel that fits the width, chop the mortises in both jaws, working from each edge. Otherwise, bore a ½" hole, then pare the waste to the line.

Ensure that the arms fit tightly in the front jaw mortises but have a little play in the rear jaw. I like to use a rasp to open up the rear jaw mortises a little.

Bevel the outside edge of the front jaw. Plane a ⅜" x ⅜" rabbet along the top back edge of the rear jaw. Smooth plane the faces, then break all the outside corners on the jaws. Slide the arms through the rear jaw and into the front jaw. Line up the end of the arm so that it slightly proud of the reference face.

Bore ⅜" peg holes through the fixed front jaw and the arms. Make two roughly rounded ⅜"-thick pegs from the arm waste you sawed away earlier. Check one final time to ensure that the rear jaw slides smoothly on the arms and make any necessary adjustments.

Finally, drive the pegs home into the peg holes and make any final adjustments to the wedges to ensure they hold tight. Give the entire piece a couple of coats of wiping varnish to complete the project.

USING THE RAAMTANG

If you've seen the Moxon vise in action, you are familiar with many of the things of which this type of vise is capable.

I have used the raamtang in conjunction with my holdfasts to dovetail case sides, a task at which it excels. I have also used it to help keep boards aligned while gluing them into wide panels.

Line it up. Note that the bottom of the rabbet aligns with the top edge of the arm mortises.

Side action. Clamping the sides of the piece being mortised helps prevent cheek blowout.

Working out. Here's the task for which the raamtang was designed—holding small pieces of molding for planing.

This vise also is an excellent appliance to hold and support a workpiece while cutting a mortise; clamping along the outside helps to prevent you from blowing out the side of the mortise with the chisel.

As you might expect, given that this was originally designed as a joiner's appliance (namely for holding window pieces for shaping), it excels at holding stock for molding, rabbeting, and even planing grooves.

When it comes to planing the saw marks off the back of a freshly stuck piece of hand-cut molding, I've yet to find anything better.

It holds like a bear trap (especially with a bit of leather glued to the working faces), is simple to make, and costs next to nothing if you use pieces from the scrap bin. What else can you ask for from a shop appliance? ■

BENCH HOOK

The single most important hand-tool appliance is three sticks of wood.

BY CHRISTOPHER SCHWARZ

Owning a backsaw without owning a bench hook is like riding a bicycle without handlebars. This simple hand-tool appliance (three pieces of wood) uses the force of the tool and gravity to hold your work as you saw. And it helps guide your tool so your cuts are right on the line.

It also allows you to make cuts with ease that are terrifying (or should be terrifying) on a power saw. A bench hook also can serve as a shooting board for trimming the face grain and end grain of small pieces of work with the help of a handplane. Plus, building one takes minutes, not hours.

Now I wish I could tell you that I've cooked up a new design of bench hook that trumps traditional designs. I haven't. In fact, I think that's an unlikely thing to accomplish.

The only "improvement" that we moderns can offer is to make it with power equipment, which improves the long-term reliability of the bench hook. Here's what I mean:

All bench hooks have three parts: The bed, which is the flat part where you put the work; the fence, which is what you push the work against; and the hook, which lips over the front edge of your benchtop.

Early bench hooks were made from one piece of wood. The bed, fence, and hook were all sawn from a single piece of thick stock. Later bench hooks were made from three pieces of wood, but the grain of the

fence and the hook were at 90° to that of the bed, so your bench hook could self-destruct (thank you seasonal expansion and contraction) before the appliance got completely chewed up by your saw.

With the help of accurate, modern table saws, it's easy to make bench hooks so that the grain direction in all three pieces is aligned. And that's exactly what you should do. (Or even make it out of plywood.)

CUT LIST & MATERIALS						
	NO.	ITEM	DIMENSIONS (INCHES)			MATERIAL
			T	W	L	
☐	1	Bed	¾	6	8	Hardwood
☐	1	Fence	¾	5¼	2	Hardwood
☐	1	Hook	¾	6	2	Hardwood

3D VIEW

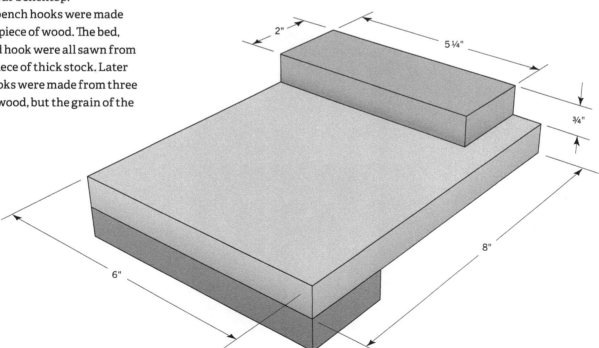

PART SIZES AND ASSEMBLY

Bench hooks can be almost any size. The sizes shown in this article make a bench hook that's convenient for most sawing. Glue and nail the three parts together, using a square to ensure the fence is square to the bed.

With your bench hook assembled, mark a scale on its fence in ½" or ¼"

increments. The scale helps you cut short bits to length. When the glue dries, you're ready to go to work. Don't apply a film finish to the bench hook; that will only make it slippery and difficult for you to keep your work in place.

Make a second bench hook without the fence. This second appliance supports long workpieces hanging off your first bench hook.

USING THE HOOK

The first rule of bench hooks: They are disposable. You will cut them up until they're unusable. So don't fret when you slice up the bed. In general, you place your work against the fence and hold it there with your off-hand while you saw with your dominant hand. As with all sawing, it's best to advance on two lines instead of one—so try to saw through an edge and a face at the same time. This trick will make all your saw cuts more accurate.

In general, I line up the edge of the bench hook's fence with the line I've marked on the wood. Lining up your fence and your cut line creates one longer line, and that's a visual cue that will help you saw straighter.

As with all sawing, allow your sawing arm the freedom to move back and forth without rubbing against your torso. That helps improve your accuracy, too.

Using a bench hook allows you to do things safely, accurately, and more quickly than with any other setup. I like to use them to cut small parts to precise lengths. I simply clamp a spring clamp to the fence at the desired dimension and butt my stock against the clamp. There's no better

Advance on two fronts. When you mark your cut line on the face of your work, wrap it around the board's edge as well. Then saw by advancing on two lines whenever you can. This greatly improves accuracy.

Shoot ends. Flip your bench hook over to use it as a small shooting board. A heavy plane with a sharp iron makes this easy. A block plane with a dull iron makes it almost impossible.

Shoot edges. The fence of your bench hook is a great planing stop when sizing small pieces. The only limitation is the thickness of the fence. It needs to be thinner than your stock. If you are going to shoot like this a lot, I'd make your fence ⅝" thick instead of ¾".

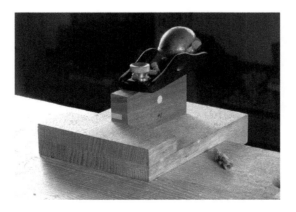

way to cut short dowels for pegging joints.

BENCH HOOKS AND PLANES

I use my bench hook with a plane just as often as I use it with a saw. When working the shoulders and cheeks of tenons with a shoulder plane, I push the work against the fence with my off-hand and plane with my dominant one.

I also use the bench hook like a small shooting board. Flip the bench hook upside down so the fence hooks over the benchtop and you are working into the hook. The extra-wide hook prevents (or reduces) blow-out on the outfeed side of your cut. Your handplane (choose a tool with lots of mass) rides on your benchtop. Butt your stock against the sole of the plane, then push the plane forward to shave off a little bit of the work. This is a great way to fit mullions in a divided-light door.

You also can use the bench hook to plane the long grain of short pieces. Push the part's end grain against the fence of the bench hook and plane away. This is easier than trying to secure little bits in your vise.

Once you have made a couple bench hooks, you'll start using them to hold your work instead of reaching for a clamp. I secure stuff against them for chiseling and rasping all the time.

Most important, I think you'll like your backsaw a lot more and use it for more operations. I've been in too many shops where backsaws were assumed to be freehand tools, so the resident woodworker was either a highly skilled sawyer or a highly frustrated one. ■

Handscrew serves as length stop

Bench hook

Cutting small pieces. Cutting short pieces to accurate length is a tricky operation with a miter saw. The bench hook, backsaw, and a handscrew clamp make the job safe and efficient.

Work

Bench hook

Scrap protects side of plane and raises its cutter

Shooting board. The bench hook makes an effective shooting board for truing the ends of small pieces. The piece of scrap below the plane protects the side of the tool and centers the tool's cutter on the work.

CONTRIBUTORS

Master Cabinetmaker's Bench (p. 38)
Frank Rohrbach, Illustrator
Mario Rodriquez, Photographer
Tom Caspar, Editor

Knockdown English Workbench (p. 62)
Al Parrish, Lead Photographer
Christopher Schwarz, Photographer
Louis Bois, Illustrator
Mike Siemsen, Sidebar Author

I-Beam Work Island (p. 112)
Al Parrish, Photographer

A Bench for Kids (p. 131)
Jameel Abraham, Photographer

Workbench Enrichment (p. 148)
Al Parrish, Photographer

Bench Deadman (p. 156)
Al Parrish, Photographer
Christopher Schwarz, Author

Shop-Made Tail Vise (p. 166)
Christopher Schwarz, Photographer
Robert W. Lang, Illustrator

Bench Hook (p. 181)
Al Parrish, Photographer

TOOLS, SUPPLIES & RESOURCES

Visit your local woodworking store or look online for these brands mentioned in the book.

Bark House (kiln-dried lumber slabs) barkhouse.com

Beall Tool Co. (wood threading kit) bealltool.com

Benchcrafted (vises) benchcrafted.com

Black + Decker (Workmate) blackanddecker.com

DELTA (table saws) deltamachinery.com

Dieter Schmid Fine Tools (tools, work-holding) fine-tools.com

Festool (DOMINO jointer) festoolusa.com

Freud (table saw blades) freudtools.com

Gramercy Tools (holdfasts) toolsforworkingwood.com

Kreg Tool (pocket screws, jigs) kregtool.com

Loctite (thread-locking anaerobic glue) loctiteproducts.com

Olde Century Colors (paint) oldecenturycolors.com

Southern Pine (yellow pine) southernpine.com

The Real Milk Paint Co. (milk paint) realmilkpaint.com

Ulmia (workbenches) ulmia.de/ulmia-en

Woodhaven (T-track) woodhaven.com

Woodmizer (local sawyer directory) woodmizer.com/us/Find-a-Local-Sawyer

INDEX

Text and photographs © 2022

Publisher: Paul McGahren
Editorial Director: Kerri Grzybicki
Design & Layout: Clare Finney

Cedar Lane Press
PO Box 5424
Lancaster, PA 17606-5424

Paperback ISBN: 978-1-950934-88-1
ePub ISBN: 978-1-950934-89-8

Library of Congress Control Number: 2022945132

Printed in the United States of America
10 9 8 7 6 5 4 3 2 1

Note: The following list contains names used in *Make Your Own Workbench* that may be registered with the United States Copyright Office:

Appleply; Beall Tool Co.; Benchcrafted (Hi Vise); Black + Decker (Workmate); "Car Talk"; DELTA (UNISAW); DeWalt; Four Centuries of Dutch Planes and Planemakers; Festool (DOMINO); Hammacher, Schlemmer & Co.; Henkel Corporation (Loctite); IRWIN; *L'Art du Menuisier*; Lost Arts Press *(The Woodworker, Volume 4)*; Philadelphia Furniture Workshop; *Popular Woodworking*; SketchUp; Southern Forest Products Association (Southern Pine); *Tage Frid Teaches Woodworking; The Art of the Woodworker*; The Real Milk Paint Co.; *Traditional Woodworking Handtools; Woodworking in Estonia; Workbenches: From Design & Theory to Construction & Use.*

To learn more about Cedar Lane Press books, or to find a retailer near you, email info@cedarlanepress.com or visit us at www.cedarlanepress.com.

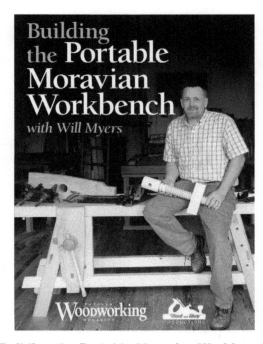
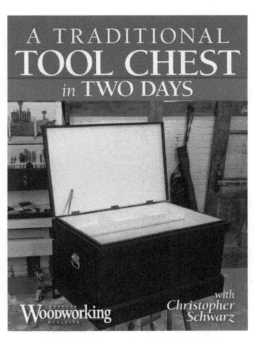

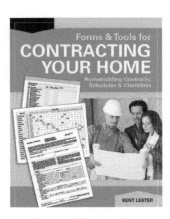
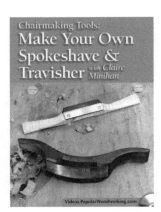

CPSIA information can be obtained
at www.ICGtesting.com
Printed in the USA
JSHW051629111222
34694JS00001B/1

9 781950 934881